The Life and Times of
CHARLES II

The Life and Times of
CHARLES II

Christopher Falkus

Introduction by Antonia Fraser

CROSS RIVER PRESS
A division of Abbeville Press, Inc.
NEW YORK

First published in the United States, 1992,
by Cross River Press, a division of Abbeville
Press, Inc., 488 Madison Avenue, New York,
NY 10022.

First published in the United Kingdom, 1972,
by George Weidenfeld and Nicolson Ltd.

© George Weidenfeld and Nicolson Limited
and Book Club Associates 1972, 1992

Series designed by Paul Watkins

ISBN 1-55859-446-9

Contents

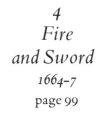

Introduction

A<small>TTRACTIVE</small>, <small>LAZY</small>, <small>SENSUAL</small>, has King Charles II had, perhaps, too good a press from the English public? We think with admiring tolerance of 'Good King Charles's Golden Days' – associated as they are with the Restoration Court and all the name implies of high living and rather lower moral standards, and royal mistresses galore from Nell Gwynne, the saucy actress, to the Frenchwoman Louise de Kéroualle who became an English Duchess. It is possible that some sterner judgment might be in order?

The clue to the reign certainly lies in the character of King Charles himself. He came to the throne, after all, at a most critical moment for the monarchy, dispossessed for the last eleven years, and found himself ruling over an England which had been divided not only by the Civil War but also by the establishment of a republican regime. The Royalists had suffered penalties quite sufficient to breed a spirit of vengeance among his supporters who now, in 1660, returned behind the King in triumph. In this context it was of the utmost importance that King Charles was a man, in the words of the Marquis of Halifax, full of inclinations to give and to forgive.

Yet by the end of Charles's reign twenty-five years later, it was easier to subscribe to the other half of Halifax's judgment: the King possessed 'gifts rather than virtues'. His foreign policy had ultimately concentrated on receiving heavy subsidies from the French King Louis XIV in order to render himself independent of his own Parliament; and from whose interference he never found a more practical escape than ruling in effect without it. A man who certainly died a Roman Catholic, and was sympathetic to the cause of the Catholic Church throughout his life, he was nevertheless unable to halt the mayhem of the Popish Plot; nor was State tolerance of religious minorities increased during his reign. A convinced upholder of the principles of monarchy, he found himself unable to take steps to leave behind him the legitimate heir who might have saved England from the troubles so obviously inherent in the rule of his brother James II. And it was one of his illegitimate sons, the Duke of Monmouth, who attempted to seize James's throne in the months after his death.

It is arguable however that these sterner judgements of historical realities are as unfair to 'good King Charles' as the popular notion of his golden reign; they allow too little for the healing balm of this affable monarch at a most difficult period of transition in our history. At least a sort of peace prevailed, in contrast to the turbulence both before and after. It is one of the merits of Christopher Falkus's energetically-written and enjoyable biography that while these political issues are discussed and estimated with clarity, the King himself never loses his personality. We do not forget that Charles – of all the Stuarts – never lost the 'common touch' for which we still admire him; perhaps after all that was the quality most necessary to a King coming to the throne in 1660.

Antonia Fraser

THE KING *was inferior to none, either in shape or air; his wit was pleasant; his disposition easy and affable; his soul, susceptible of opposite impressions, was compassionate to the unhappy, inflexible to the wicked and tender even to excess; ... his heart was often the dupe, but oftener the slave, of his attachments.*

ANTHONY HAMILTON

FORGIVING, *humble, bounteous, just and kind:*
  His conversation, wits and parts,
His knowledge in the noblest useful arts,
Were such dead authors could not give,
But habitudes of those who live ...
His apprehension quick, his judgement true;
That the most learn'd, with shame, confess
His knowledge more, his reading only less.

JOHN DRYDEN

1 A Lost Inheritance
1630-49

M AY THE 29th, 1630 was a day of rejoicing for a troubled nation. Shortly before midday Henrietta Maria, Charles I's French and Roman Catholic wife, gave birth to a fine healthy son, and all over London bonfires were lit, bells were rung, and men raised their glasses to the new Prince of Wales. It was good to have an heir born in England, even if he was of a French mother and a Scottish father. Astrologers noted happily that the portents were favourable. All day long the planet Venus was visible to the naked eye, though none could have guessed the scale of the endowment bestowed on the baby Prince by the goddess of love.

At St James's Palace the event was treated more calmly, and with due regard to precedent and time-honoured custom. Lords and ladies provided the necessary witnesses of delivery, and the baby was removed to apartments already prepared and supplied with a suitable retinue: a governess, a wet-nurse, a dry-nurse and half-a-dozen ladies to rock the royal cradle. When the time came for him to be baptised, the sacrament was administered by the King's favourite bishop, William Laud of London, who duly christened him Charles after his father. Given all the attention appropriate to the heir to the throne and the hope of the dynasty the baby flourished, and the Queen was soon writing to a friend: 'He is so fat and so tall that he is taken for a year old and he is only four months. His teeth are already beginning to come. I will send you his portrait as soon as he is a little fairer, for at present he is so dark that I am ashamed of him.' Charles was, however, never to lose his dark complexion, and years later 'the black boy' still clung to him as a nickname.

By all accounts young Charles was not precocious. He was forward only in his disposition to be demonstratively affectionate to those around him, a tendency which did not altogether leave him in later life. His playmates at St James's included the daughter and two sons of the Duke of Buckingham, his father's former favourite and evil genius who had been assassinated in 1628; while younger brothers and sisters arrived periodically to join him in the nursery – Mary, after a year, James, after three, followed by Elizabeth, Anne and Henry. It was a happy atmosphere in which to grow from infancy to boyhood, and life became no less pleasant when, at the age of eight, it was time to give him his own court at Richmond and to take him out of the

PREVIOUS PAGES Charles I and Henrietta Maria, painted by Daniel Mytens in 1634.

LEFT Charles and Henrietta Maria with their two eldest children, Charles, Prince of Wales, born in 1630, and Mary, born in 1631. Painting by Anthony van Dyck.

13

REGIS MAGNÆ BRITANIÆ
PROLES
PRINCEPS CAROLVS NATVS 2 NOV 631
JACOBVS DVX EBORACENSIS NAT 15 OCTOB
ET FILIA PRINCEPS MARIA NATA 4 NO 631

Charles with his sister
Mary, who became
Princess of Orange, and
his brother James, Duke
of York. Painting by
Van Dyck.

15

Charles was given his own court at Richmond Palace when he was eight.
The old palace, built by Henry VII, from an etching by Wenceslaus Hollar.

hands of women and entrust him to the care of a governor. The man chosen for the task was, naturally enough, a nobleman of the highest rank. The importance of the Earl of Newcastle's appointment lies in the fact that so many of his own qualities and characteristics were later to be evident in his pupil. The Earl was courteous, kindly, optimistic by nature and supremely conscious of the qualities which went to create a gentleman.

Among these, scholarship was not rated highly, but good manners and good horsemanship were important. Some of Newcastle's injunctions to his pupil are guides to Charles's developing character: 'I would not have you too studious, for too much contemplation spoils action'; 'The things that I have discoursed to you most is to be courteous and civil to everybody; and believe it, the putting off of your hat and making a leg

RICHMOND

W. Hollar real 1078

18

pleases more than reward or preservation.' And, 'to women you cannot be too civil, especially to great ones.' Charles was to follow Newcastle's advice and example closely. He retained a lively curiosity in many fields, but nobody thought of him as studious; he was most attentive to the ladies, and, like his mentor, became an enthusiastic sportsman. Later on he was to have other governors, the bookish Marquis of Hertford and the ineffectual Earl of Berkshire, but Newcastle was the only one who made any real impact on his early development.

Nor did Charles owe much to his parents, who were usually too preoccupied with affairs of State at Whitehall to pay much attention to the children. It is remarkable how few of the traits of either young Charles inherited. Both were fervently religious, the King matching his wife's Catholicism with an equal devotion

ABOVE William Cavendish, Earl of Newcastle, from an engraving by Van Dyck. Newcastle became Charles's governor in 1638 and he was very influential in the development of the Prince's character.
LEFT The model of a ship made by Phineas Pett in 1634, and given to Charles.
OPPOSITE Charles at the age of twelve, a portrait by Dobson. Despite his youth, his martial qualities are shown, as he crushes Medusa.

to the Anglican Church. Charles I was a loving and faithful husband, austere in his personal life, inflexible in political outlook. Henrietta was strong-willed, ambitious and formidably business-like. All this was very different from the worldly, tolerant, easy-going personality which was to characterise their eldest son. He owed it, perhaps not only to Newcastle but to the blood of his great ancestor Henry of Navarre, his grandfather on his mother's side, and a King of France who knew the art of compromise.

It was an art concealed from Charles I, and it was a misfortune for ruler and ruled alike that the reign of such a man should have coincided with changes which required a more subtle touch than Charles's to keep the peace. For what was happening was nothing less than a shift in the balance of power within the nation at the expense of the Crown, something which was to have the profoundest of effects on the reign not only of the father but of the son as well.

The visible aspects of these changes, important though they were, would not have been obvious even to the older inhabitants of the kingdom. Outwardly Stuart England differed little from the kingdom of the Tudors. It was still sparsely peopled, for though the population was increasing, the total was probably only some four million at the time of young Charles's birth. London, with about half a million, remained the only sizeable town, and even in the capital the fields were nowhere far away. Of the other towns the greatest, such as Bristol and Norwich, were no more than fair-sized villages, while the overwhelming majority of people farmed their living from the land as they had done since time out of mind. The land itself looked very much as it always had done, for though some progressive farmers had enclosed their fields with those hedges so characteristic of the countryside today, England for the most part still consisted of vast tracts of open territory: much of it forested, much of it waste, much of it in common use for grazing, and, where the soil was suitable, some of it farmed in narrow strips as had been the custom since before the Conquest.

Nevertheless this apparently stable kingdom, and the society which it supported, was developing in ways which at least the more perceptive were able to recognise. Already some fifty years earlier, one Englishman had written: 'There are old men

20

yet dwelling in the village where I remain, which have noted three things to be marvellously altered.' He was referring to the growing number of chimneys which were everywhere in evidence; the increasing use of proper bedding and pillows; and the change from wooden plates and dishes to those of pewter, silver and tin. These were signs of the times, of a gradual social and economic transformation which was to underlie much of the tragic history of the Stuarts. For, in an age of rising prices and profits, and of expanding population and trade, the Crown was ill-equipped to keep pace with its wealthier subjects. Depending as it did on traditional sources of revenue and on taxes squeezed out of reluctant Parliaments, it was forced to part with much of its land, and this made its long-term financial plight worse. Meanwhile, those who enjoyed the wealth and paid the taxes – whether peers or commoners – felt, not unnaturally, that they should share in the business of government which historically belonged to the King and his chosen ministers. The public forum of their discontent was Parliament, and much of Charles II's reign, like that of his father, was to be a running fight with successive Parliaments which demanded a voice in the affairs of State as the price of their grants of money. A year before the Prince's birth, there had been an ugly scene in the Commons when angry members had refused to disband, holding the Speaker in his chair while resolutions about their grievances were put to the House. Thereupon the King had resolved to manage without Parliament altogether, and to rule as best he could with the aid of loyal ministers. It was a decision which wrecked any hope of co-operation between the King and his most influential subjects. Outside the immediate circle of the court and its officials, the chief ministers – Thomas Wentworth, Earl of Strafford, and Laud, now Archbishop of Canterbury – were widely detested. The arbitrary nature of their government, their taxes, their unwillingness to consult – these were discontents steadily breeding a revolution. Popular leaders such as John Pym and John Hampden came forward to speak out against the regime, and it is not altogether fanciful to imagine that their names were known to the children at St James's as nursery bogeymen, much as Hitler became a bogeyman to a later generation of children.

As usual in times of crisis, ideology became intertwined with more material grievances. Ever since the reign of Bloody Mary, when three hundred Protestants had perished for their faith, Englishmen had dreaded the return of the Catholics to power. The Gunpowder Plot was a recent memory, and nothing was more calculated to appeal to the deepest prejudices of the nation than the cry of Popery in high places. Now resentment was focussed not only on the Queen and her Catholic entourage, but on the High Church Anglicanism of the King and his bishops. Increasingly the opposition attacked the whole panoply of the Church hierarchy, and many of the most outspoken favoured the Presbyterian system of elected ministers and elders which had no Popish connotations. In short, the nation was politically and spiritually torn apart, and Charles I was incapable of carrying out his self-appointed task of preserving intact the monarchy of his predecessors and the inheritance which would one day be his son's.

The King could delay a showdown as long as he could avoid meeting a Parliament. And for eleven years he managed to do so, though each year that passed made it less likely that he would emerge unscathed should circumstances compel him once again to summon his Lords and Commons. At last, in 1638, he made his fatal mistake. A disastrous attempt to impose an English-style Prayer Book on the Presbyterian Scots led to a war which bankrupted his government and, with his troops routed, left him no option but to seek fresh supplies from the assembly he had tried so hard to do without.

Young Charles was not quite ten when the first Parliament of his lifetime met in April 1640. The state opening enchanted the diarist John Evelyn who wrote of the 'very glorious and magnificent sight, the king encircled with his royal diadem and the affections of his people'. It was an illusion. In three weeks this shambles, known to history as the Short Parliament, was dissolved in a welter of accusations and recriminations, and the writs went out for a new one, summoned for November. But this time there could be no abrupt dismissal; the Scots were in possession of the English border counties and exacting a huge ransom under threat of moving further south. The new Parliament would have to take its course, and when the returns came in it was apparent that victory belonged to the declared enemies of the government.

The trial of Thomas Wentworth, Earl of Strafford, which took place in spring 1641, in the House of Lords. After the Earl had been found guilty of treason, Charles I sought to save him by sending the Prince of Wales with a message to the Lords. But the plea was ignored, and Strafford was executed the following day on Tower Hill.

The Long Parliament, which lasted in a variety of forms for the next twenty years, accomplished a political revolution. The pent-up frustrations of many years resulted in an outburst of legislation aimed at preventing the helpless King from dispensing with Parliamentary services again. Strafford and Laud were sent to the Tower: ancient Crown revenues dating back to feudal times were abolished; and a law was passed to ensure that a new Parliament would be summoned once every three years.

All this could scarcely have been understood by the young Prince, though for the nation it marked a real break with a personal system of monarchy which had its roots deep in antiquity. But there was one event which must have remained with Charles as a memory for the rest of his life. The mood of Parliament was such that a victim was inevitable, and the chief target was Strafford, ablest of the King's ministers. He was impeached in the House of Commons for treason, but defended himself so well that it was decided to proceed by a Bill of Attainder, that is to say simply by a Parliamentary Bill declaring the Earl to be guilty. In the spring of 1641 the Lords debated the Bill, their deliberations often witnessed by the King from his curtained box in the company of his eldest son. At length it was passed and, after an agony of indecision, the King gave the royal assent. But, having signed away the life of the best servant he ever had, Charles now sought to save it with a letter pleading for the Earl's life. The chosen messenger was the Prince of Wales, not quite eleven years old. It was a strange scene, the little Prince gorgeously decked out in robes of State passing through the ranks of the silent peers, delivering his message to the magisterial Lord Keeper of the Great Seal, and solemnly withdrawing through the same silent ranks. After his departure there was a moment of uneasy silence. Then somebody moved that they pass on to the next business. The next day, 12 May, Strafford was beheaded on Tower Hill.

The death of Strafford did not satisfy the government's critics, and some of them were encouraged to press for far more extravagant demands, for Parliamentary control of the Church, of the King's ministers and of the armed forces. Such demands went far beyond the ambitions of more moderate men who up to this point had belonged to the opposition. It was now apparent that something highly significant was happening, a Royalist reaction and the growth of a King's Party. The King in his turn was encouraged, and throughout the spring and summer of 1642 positions on either side were being strengthened in preparation for battle.

Among those who left the opposition to join the King was the lawyer Edward Hyde, very fat, very able, pompous in manner but moderate enough to be appalled at the extremism of his more fanatical colleagues. He rose quickly in the councils of the King and was one of those who left London when it became obvious that the capital was too dangerous a place for Royalists. The Queen was sent off to the safety of Holland while the Royalist Party – the Cavaliers as they were soon to be known – moved into the countryside to gather support. On 19 August 1642 they raised their battle standard at Nottingham. It was the signal for the opening of the Civil War.

For the royal brothers Charles and James, now twelve and nine respectively, the first phase of the war was a time of intense excitement. They had their own parts to play, moving in and out of the brightly-coloured ranks which were being assembled, graciously acknowledging the loyal cheers they received. Above all there was the boys' hero and cousin, dashing Prince Rupert, whose cavalry exploits gave promise of an early victory for the Royalists. Both boys witnessed the first battle of the war at Edgehill, standing dangerously near the falling cannon balls in the company of the great physician William Harvey, who was too engrossed in his book to pay them much attention. These were stirring times, made all the more thrilling by the apparent certainty of Royalist success.

Charles spent much of the time at his father's side, either at his headquarters in Oxford or following the Royalist armies on their campaigns. But though there were successes there was no final victory, and gradually even the successes became less frequent. By 1644 a new force was in the field, the cavalry of 'Ironsides' recruited from the eastern counties, trained and led by the burly, ruddy-faced member for Cambridge, Oliver Cromwell. The Ironsides soon showed their worth, shattering Prince Rupert's army at Marston Moor on 2 July. The Royalists were becoming discouraged, and to revive their spirits the King decided to 'unboy' his son, despatching him to Bristol

Prince Rupert, Count
Palatine of the Rhine and
Duke of Bavaria. Exiled
from Bohemia in 1619, he
came to Charles I's
assistance during the Civil
War and led the cavalry of
the Royalist army. His
cavalry exploits made
him the greatest of the
Royalist heroes.

early in 1645 to take command of all his forces in the West. The Prince was delighted, and even the solid downpour of rain in which he made the journey could not diminish his enthusiasm.

His command at Bristol lasted a year, and during it he discovered that his job was in reality not to lead but to listen as the members of his Council – such as Culpeper, Hopton and Berkshire – quarrelled and debated endlessly among themselves. Overshadowing them all was the voluble Hyde, keeping the fifteen-year-old Prince firmly in his place. But, had his Council been less factious, there was little enough which could have been done to save the Stuart cause. In the summer the Parliamentarians won another crushing victory at Naseby, and by Christmas the King was writing to his son urging him to prepare his escape. Soon the Parliamentary armies were moving

Oliver Cromwell, Lord Protector of England. He became the most successful general of the Roundhead army during the Civil War. Cromwell was one of the signatories to Charles I's death warrant and became Lord Protector in 1653. Thereafter he ruled the country as virtual dictator, up to his death in 1658.

west, Charles and his advisers retreating before them. At last they sought refuge in Pendennis Castle in Cornwall, where they heard news of the final Royalist defeat at Torrington. There was no alternative but flight, and at ten o'clock on the night of 2 March 1646 a dispirited and destitute band slipped away on board the *Phoenix* for the Scillies where they spent six miserable weeks desperately short of money, food and clothes. Their plight is well described by one of the Royalist ladies in the group:

> After being pillaged, and extremely sick, I was set on shore almost dead in the island of Scilly. When we had got to our quarters near the Castle, where the Prince lay, I went immediately to bed, which was so vile, that my footman ever lay in a better, and we had but three in the whole house, which consisted of four rooms, or rather partitions, two low rooms and two little lofts, with a ladder to go up; in one of these they kept dried fish, which was his trade, and in this my husband's two clerks lay, one there was for my sister, and one for myself, and one amongst the rest of the servants. But, when I waked in the morning, I was so cold I knew not what to do, but the daylight discovered that my bed was near swimming with the sea, which the owner told us afterward it never did so but at spring-tide. With this, we were destitute of clothes, and meat, and fuel, for half the Court to serve them for a month was not to be had in the whole island; and truly we begged our daily bread of God, for we thought every meal our Last.

The Scillies were clearly not to be tolerated for long, and on 16 April they embarked again, this time for Jersey, one of the few parts of the King's dominions still loyal to the Stuarts.

It was a sad little party that arrived in Jersey, only Charles showing that astonishing resilience – even indifference – to misfortune which was becoming one of his most enduring characteristics. While his companions fretted, he busied himself learning to sail and making suggestions for improving the island's fortifications. He delighted the populace by his familiarity, and it was a regular spectacle to watch him dine, surrounded by his gentlemen-in-waiting, with a doctor of theology to say grace, a page on one knee to present his basin and napkin, an attendant to taste every dish before passing it to the Prince, and another to hold a silver plate under the royal chin when he drank. By this time Charles was developing rapidly out of his adolescence, and though not conventionally handsome, there is no doubt that the tall dark youth, with his heavy features and sensual mouth was already attractive to women. And he was returning the interest. There is some reason to believe that he may have enjoyed his first affair with his former governess, Mrs Wyndham, while in the West Country: and in Jersey, it was said, he flirted with the pretty Margaret de Carteret, kinswoman of the island's Governor.

But whatever delights Charles discovered in Jersey, they could not sustain him for long, and soon a slightly bored young Prince was casting his eyes in a different direction. From France his mother was calling him to join her, rosily describing the pleasures which awaited him there. From England his hapless father was urging the same course, fearful that the island defences offered slim protection against the Parliamentary fleet. Charles's advisers were not convinced, arguing that the morale of the Royalists would be damaged if he were to leave the royal dominions but, doubtless to their surprise, they found themselves overruled by their youthful master, and on 26 June, he landed in France with a handful of councillors – though not Hyde, who remained obstinately in Jersey – a considerable retinue of servants, excited and impatient to begin his new adventure.

In a short life already patterned with unfulfilled hopes, France was yet another disappointment. Charles's reception was not at all what he had been led to expect. He lodged modestly with his mother at her headquarters in St Germain, and for some two months was not even permitted to attend the court at Fontainebleau. Once there, he fitted uneasily into the stiffly formal atmosphere which surrounded his eight-year-old cousin, Louis XIV, and he remained a shy, unimportant outsider. France's chief minister, Cardinal Mazarin, had little use for a figure of such political insignificance, while financially he was dependent on his mother. That forbidding lady made certain that he played little part in the councils of the exiles, and he was not allowed to read the documents presented to him for signature. She even pocketed the small pension granted by the French court, arguing that it was humiliating for Charles to be a pensioner of France. Worse than this she extended her domain into the realm of her son's private life, producing what she considered to be a most suitable candidate for a prospective daughter-in-law.

The lady in question was Anne-Marie-Louise, daughter of Gaston, Duc d'Orléans, and the richest heiress in Europe. Nineteen years old, opinionated, enormously confident of her importance, beauty and intelligence, she had no intention of marrying so poor a catch as the penniless heir to an uncertain throne. It was not that she found him totally unattractive, though 'big enough for his age, good-looking head, black hair, dark complexion and passably good looking' was the limit of her enthusiasm. It was simply that her sights were on bigger game, preferably the Holy Roman Emperor but failing him the King of Spain. Charles did not stand a chance; nor did he want to. But for his mother's sake he went through the motions of his supposed grand passion. 'La Grande Mademoiselle', as she was known to everyone, wrote: 'he never failed to place himself beside me. When I visited the Queen he conducted me in his coach; and whatever the weather might be, he held his hat in his hand until he had left me. His courtesy to me was apparent in the smallest things.'

The Prince, in short, did everything to ingratiate himself except make a declaration of his love. Here the courtship foundered on Charles's inability, or unwillingness, to speak French and Mademoiselle's to understand English. His mother explained to the slightly piqued girl that her son was struck dumb by the depth of his feelings; a clever but unconvincing excuse since he was clearly capable of finding sufficient phrases to indulge in the variety of more congenial amours in which he sought relief.

Charles, in fact, was better off than those of his companions who chafed at their inactivity. Their Prince could always find diversions, whether conducting the scientific experiments which were such a popular amateur pastime of the age, studying mathematics with the redoubtable Thomas Hobbes, or seeking his more earthy pleasures in such willing company as that of his old playmate from the nursery, George Villiers, second Duke of Buckingham. His mother placed no restrictions on these matters and the exiles – led by such rakes as Buckingham, Jermyn, Percy and the Prince himself – gained an unenviable reputation for idleness and debauchery. When the gallant James

Graham, better known to history as the Marquis of Montrose, joined them from Scotland he was scandalised by the 'lewdness and worthlessness' of the court and took no part in its proceedings.

The strictures were no doubt justified, but it is difficult to see what in any case could have been done to influence events across the Channel. Montrose himself had worked wonders with a small band of clansmen to prop up the ailing Royalist cause; but even he had been forced to flee before his enemies. Now he was as helpless as the others as news arrived from England. It was a grim story: of the King's surrender to the Scots; of his being handed over to Parliament; of his flight to the Isle of Wight and frantic attempts to persuade the Scots to come to his rescue; of Cromwell's crushing defeat of the Scottish army at Preston, and the final eclipse of these hopes.

All this made little impact on the round of balls, masques and plays which comprised so much of the exiles' routine. But the pattern was broken in the summer of 1648 when a Parliamentary fleet turned itself over to the Royalists, and it seemed that at last there was the possibility of action. Charles joined it in Holland, and assumed nominal command to the intense disappointment of his fifteen-year-old brother James, Duke of York. James had only recently arrived, following a spectacular escape from England disguised as a girl, and as titular Lord High Admiral he resented being superseded. Charles took no notice of his brother's annoyance and was soon at sea, searching for the enemy fleet commanded by the Earl of Warwick. He was anxious for combat, once seizing a gun and declaring that with it he would put a bullet through Warwick's head. But there was no battle, and adverse winds compelled the Royalist ships to return to Holland where they were disbanded amidst mutinous murmurings from the crews who had expected a profitable voyage of plunder and prizes.

Charles was disappointed, but found consolation of a kind which never failed to distract him from more sombre thoughts. At the Hague he had already encountered a young English refugee called Lucy Walter, and now the affair was resumed. Lucy was of Welsh origin; Evelyn found her 'a brown, beautiful, bold but insipid creature', and there can be little doubt that Charles fell genuinely in love. The son she bore in April he

'Big enough for his age ... and passably good looking'

31

32

'To Kill a King'

LEFT Charles I during his trial. His last portrait was painted by Edward Bower. RIGHT When the Prince of Wales heard that his father was being tried for his life, he sent Parliament a *carte blanche*, a piece of paper blank except for his signature, so that the terms for saving the King's life could be written in. BELOW This gesture failed, and on 30 January 1649, Charles I was executed.

33

34

OPPOSITE Lucy Walter, whom Charles first met as an English refugee at The Hague. She became Charles's mistress in April 1649, and bore him a son, James, later Duke of Monmouth. Lucy died impoverished and neglected in 1657, and was never to enjoy the benefits of Charles's restoration to the throne. She is depicted here with the portrait of her son.
LEFT A miniature by Samuel Cooper of James Scott, Duke of Monmouth and Buccleuch, Charles's first and best-loved son.

acknowledged as his own, and young James, as he was christened, remained the favourite and best-loved of his children. It was a fateful birth, for as Duke of Monmouth the child was destined to play a dramatic and tragic role in a later period of English history.

Before the son was born, another tragedy was drawing to its close at Whitehall. The news that his father was to be tried for his life sent Charles hurrying to the Dutch authorities imploring their intervention. He wrote letters to the courts of Europe, and one to the English Parliament offering any terms if the King's life were spared, enclosing with it a sheet of paper, blank save for his signature, on which those terms could be written. It was a moving gesture, more eloquent than words: but Charles I was not to be saved. In January he was tried and convicted of treason; on the 30th of that month the executioner's axe took a King from his people and a father from his son. Young Charles remained in ignorance for some days: then one of his chaplains addressed him as 'Your Majesty'. In one moment the full realisation of his father's fate flooded over him, and the new King ran sobbing to his chamber.

35

Le Blond excud auec Priuilege du Roy   Bosse in et fe.

Qui ne desireroit estre tout couuert dyeux   Chacunes a leur tour elles entrent au Bal   C'est en telle assemblee ou les di
  Pour bien considerer les beautez de ces Dames   Au son des violons qui donnent la cadence .   Rauissent les Espris, la vûe, et le
Qui parent ce Balet: leurs regards et leurs flames   L'oeil obserue attentif celle qui le mieux dance   Ou Venus s'entretient, ou les bou
Peuuent vaincre les cœurs des hommes et des dieux.   Auecque plus de grace: ou celle qui faict mal .   Content a leurs amans libremen

Si l'Amour quelque part baftit fon Paradis,
C'eft ou l'on faict Balet, on y void faces d'Anges
Au lieu d'Aftres la joye y eft dans les meflanges
D'Ebats et paffetemps plus grands qui ne font dits.

2 The Wanderer 1649-60

38

CHARLES HAD NOT KNOWN his father well enough to grieve deeply or for long. But it would be wrong to underestimate the effect of the execution on his developing character. Already his life had been crowded with events that seemed to conspire to remove every prop of security. His happy childhood had been invaded by the uncertainties of civil war; he had seen men proclaiming their loyalty to the Crown in arms against his father; he had seen his inheritance snatched from him; and now, in an age when most people still believed that kings ruled by Divine Right and were answerable for their actions only to God, he knew that even the sacred person of the Sovereign was not inviolate against forces calculated to upset every value, every assumption, which he had been taught to accept.

To the heir to the throne, above all people, regicide was more than judicial murder: it was a combination of every blasphemy, heresy and sacrilege against a man who was his King, his father, and the representative of God. The character of the young man who was emerging from these battle-scars – the cynic, the sceptic, the opportunist, who distrusted high-sounding principles as much as he sought to make the most of one night's pleasure – should surprise nobody, unless the surprise is that his spirit was not broken altogether.

But his spirit did not break and the immediate task before him was revenge. The crowned heads of Europe, appalled at the fate which had overtaken one of their number, hastened to recognise the son as Charles II. Even republican Holland was shocked into doing the same. Among the exiles there was a new sense of urgency, led by Charles himself who began to act increasingly like a King. His mother was surprised and hurt to find him appointing a Privy Council without reference to her. The indefatigable Hyde, now back with the court, surfaced from his mountains of correspondence to find Charles more difficult to handle at the meetings which ranged over the various plans of action. Montrose had just one ambition, promising the dead King:

> I'll sing thine obsequies with trumpet sounds
> And write thine epitaph in blood and wounds.

The practical possibilities were two: Charles could either place himself at the head of a Catholic army in Ireland or a

PREVIOUS PAGES
Charles II dancing at a ball at The Hague during his exile. Engraving by A. Bosse.

OPPOSITE James Graham, first Marquis of Montrose, in a painting after Honthorst. Montrose was the leader of the Royalist party in Scotland in the Civil War.

39

Presbyterian one in Scotland; for the executioner's axe had fallen on the sovereign of not one but three kingdoms, and the Irish and the Scots were outraged at the fate of their King. Scots commissioners hurried to Charles's court, where their impressions of the new King were distinctly favourable. One of them, Robert Baillie, wrote: 'He is one of the most gentle, innocent, well-inclined Princes, so far as yet appears, that lives in the world; a trim person and of manly carriage; understands pretty well; speaks not much; he might make, with God's blessing, as good a King as Britain saw these hundred years. Would God he were amongst us!'

But Charles was not so impressed with them. They were in no sense Cavaliers, but represented the narrow-minded Presbyterian clique which dominated the northern Kingdom. The Scottish leaders had sworn to a National Covenant, binding themselves to a Kirk unpolluted by bishops and priests. They criticised the pleasure-living companions with whom Charles had surrounded himself, demanding that he should accept their Covenant and undertake to impose the Presbyterian faith in England and Ireland as well; and, above all, that Montrose, 'that fugatious man and most justly excommunicate rebel James Graham', who had so recently fought for Charles I while they were fighting against him, should be dismissed. Not surprisingly Charles, supported by Hyde, decided in favour of Ireland, held for him by the loyal Ormonde, and the Scots commissioners departed in a mood of self-righteous indignation while Charles prepared to leave Holland for Jersey to await further developments.

He left Holland with a new addition to his party, for by now Lucy's son was born. Father, mother and child travelled together, stopping *en route* at St Germain where Charles renewed his interrupted courtship with La Grande Mademoiselle. As before, the affair was conducted with apathy on both sides and the great lady was able to record her disgust at his eating habits, by the way he would 'throw himself upon a piece of beef and a shoulder of mutton'.

Charles had more to worry about than his table manners, for no sooner had he reached Jersey than news reached him of Cromwell's brilliant but ruthless campaign in Ireland which had obliterated any possibility of further hope from that quarter.

'He is one of the most gentle, innocent, well-inclined Princes . . .'

40

Many of Charles's companions were in a mood of despair, but the King was not so easily discouraged. He turned once again to the Scots whose commissioners arrived in Jersey hard on the heels of the news from Ireland. Negotiations were arduous and protracted, first in Jersey and then, in the spring of 1650, at the Dutch town of Breda. Charles was confident he would be more than a match for the Presbyterians, but little by little he was forced to give way on every point, and the forebodings of his Cavalier companions were proved only too well justified. The adventurer and rake was forced to swear the most solemn oaths to reform his manner of life and uphold a creed quite alien to himself and his loyal followers. Of course Charles had no more intention of keeping his vows than the Scots had expectations that he would. Years later Alexander Jaffray, one of the commissioners, wrote in his diary:

> We did sinfully both entangle and engage the nation and ourselves and that poor young prince to whom we were sent, making him sign and swear a covenant which we knew from clear and demonstrable reasons that he hated in his heart. He sinfully complied with what we most sinfully pressed upon him; where I must confess, to my apprehension, our sin was more than his.

But for the moment Charles and the Scots were prepared to deceive each other and themselves in the interests of reaching a settlement. Charles was not even deterred by the fate of Montrose, who had been despatched to Scotland with a commission from the new King to raise a Royalist army against the very men with whom he was negotiating. Betrayed almost at once to the devious Marquis of Argyll, Montrose suffered the grisly death of traitors – to be hanged, drawn and quartered – with words of forgiveness for his enemies and loyalty to his Prince on his lips. As his remains were posted in various parts of Scotland as a warning to would-be opponents of the Kirk, Charles was fixing his signature to a document which ran:

> I Charles, King of Great Britain, France and Ireland, do assure and declare by my solemn oath, in the presence of the almighty God the searcher of hearts, my allowance and approbations of the national covenant, and of the solemn league and covenant above written; and faithfully oblige myself to prosecute the ends thereof in my station and calling; and that I for myself and successors shall consent and agree to all acts of parliament enjoining the national

covenant and the solemn league and covenant, and fully establishing presbyterial government, the directory of worship, confession of faith and catechisms in the kingdom of Scotland as they are approved by the general assembly of this kirk and parliament of this kingdom; and that I shall give my royal assent to acts of parliament, bills, ordinances, passed or to be passed in the houses of parliament enjoining the same in the rest of my dominions: and that I shall observe these in my own practice and family, and shall never make opposition to any of these, or endeavour any change thereof.

David Leslie, first Baron Newark, in 1651. Leslie accompanied Charles and the Scottish army of invasion which marched into England to try to regain Charles's throne.

With this guarantee of bad faith safely sealed, Charles set sail for the bleak northern kingdom in the summer of 1650, only to find himself subjected at once to the most extraordinary treatment. His court at Perth was little more than a mockery. He found himself almost completely in the hands of Argyll's oligarchy and the elders of the Kirk. At all times and in all places he was exposed to the strictures of pious ministers who enjoyed nothing more than hearing him repent again and again for his sins and those of his family. He was appalled at the appetite of the Presbyterians for long sermons, once having to sit through six in a row. He was forced to part with many of his favourite companions whose politics and morals offended the high-minded Scots. In such alien surroundings Charles played his part as well as he could, on occasion staying up until the early hours with Argyll as they beat their breasts, rolled around the floor and cried aloud for forgiveness for their sins.

In the conduct of affairs, Charles was allowed no part, and with Cromwell's Ironsides marching into Scotland the Scots leaders set about putting their army in order. They did this by dismissing three thousand of the best troops as 'malignants' and replacing them with 'ministers' sons, clerks and other such sanctified creatures, who hardly ever saw or heard of any other sword than that of the Spirit'. And it was with this weapon – half army, half congregation – that the Scottish commander, David Leslie, met the Ironsides at Dunbar on 3 September. The battle was over in an hour. Three thousand Scots were killed, ten thousand captured, many to be sold in slavery to the colonial plantations. Cromwell's casualties were twenty dead and fifty-eight wounded, and it is not difficult to imagine the expression on Charles's face as he solemnly wrote to the Scottish leaders of

THE SCOTS HOLDING THEIR YOVNG KINGES NOSE TO Y GRINSTO̅NE

Come to the Grinstone Charles tis now to late
To Recolect tis preshiterian fate.

Yu Cousnant pretenders, must bee
The subiect of Somer Tradgecomedie.

Jockie

Stoope Charles

LEFT Charles's nose being
held to the grindstone by
the Scots. Charles was
appalled by the treatment
he was subjected to by the
Scottish Presbyterians.
BELOW In January 1651
the Scots agreed to crown
Charles at Scone. This was
a ceremony of some pomp
and display, although
Charles had been obliged
to endure long periods of
penance beforehand.

Huych Allaerdt Exc.

his distress that God had seen fit to punish their grievous sins with such retribution. But he did more than this. He resolved to break away from his tormentors, and, on a pretext of going hunting, escaped with three companions to try to raise a Royalist army on his own. He had not gone forty miles when he was overtaken, and returned to his humiliating captivity.

But the defeat at Dunbar, and the King's flight, known ironically as 'The Start', did have some effect on his masters. Charles was now given more freedom, the promise of the command of a new army, and of a coronation on 1 January 1651. Nothing could prevent the coronation from being an occasion of pomp and display, but the Scots ensured that there were suitable preliminaries. 22 December was declared a day of general humiliation for the nation's contempt of the Gospel, while the 26th was set aside as a special day of humiliation for the sins of the royal family. Listening to the catalogue of sins prepared for the occasion Charles was heard to murmur, 'I think I must repent, too, that ever I was born.'

Certainly the young King must have been repenting of his decision to go to Scotland, and thinking longingly of the land of his birth, where, he was convinced, thousands of loyal Cavaliers were waiting to rise against Cromwell if only their King was there to lead them. All through the spring and early summer his new army was being raised, and, by mid-summer, the decision was taken. Cromwell had manœuvred himself to the north of the Scottish army, and it was time to march away from him, into England, to test the strength of Royalist feeling.

England was another disappointment. The Scots army with Charles at its head met few signs of welcome in the English towns. Local citizens, of course, gathered in the streets to cheer, but no more loudly than was necessary with the eyes of the troops upon them. Few came to join the army as it moved through northern England into the Midlands. The reasons are not hard to find. Everyone knew the treatment in store for traitors, while Englishmen turned in disgust from an army of invading Scots just as the Cavaliers turned from a would-be King sworn to impose the Covenant. It was a disheartened force which, late in August, reached Worcester only to hear that the Parliamentary armies, sweeping down from the north, had caught up with them and were lying in wait near the town.

A year to the day after Dunbar, Cromwell destroyed his new enemies at Worcester. It was fiercely fought, 'as stiff a contest for four or five hours as ever I have seen' was Cromwell's verdict. Charles himself showed great personal bravery, but he was unable to persuade Leslie, standing off with the reserves, to enter the fight. By nightfall, there was nothing for Charles to do but join the struggling remnants of his army as they sought to escape through the one remaining gate still in their hands. And so, with a handful of noblemen and Leslie's frightened troops, Charles rode off into the night, and into six weeks crowded with enough adventures for a lifetime and with stories which he would tell and retell with unfailing enthusiasm in happier years to come.

The first necessity was to detach himself from the main body of soldiers – as conspicuous as they were useless – in their forlorn march on the high road to Scotland. 'Although I could not get them to stand by me against the enemy', Charles was to recall, 'I could not get rid of them now I had a mind to it.' Eventually, however, he saw his chance, and with a few companions – Buckingham and Lord Wilmot among them – managed to slip undetected off the main road and to separate himself from the doomed columns of troops. From now on his safety would depend not on the strength of his army but on his wits. In the weeks that followed he was a hunted fugitive in his own land: there was a price on his head and the description of the 'tall black man upwards of two yards high' was posted everywhere. Yet it is easy to imagine that the wanderer, his face blackened in disguise, his feet torn and bleeding, starting at every strange sound, was a happier man than the helpless prisoner of the Scots. At least he was learning that there were loyal Englishmen who were willing to help him in spite of the rewards of betrayal and the dangers of concealment. Their names, which would never have been known to history but for the awesome company they kept, are illuminated in this brief period when the life of the King of England was in their hands.

Among them were the Penderell brothers – five of them – simple country people and Catholics. Charles was about to learn a lot about English Catholics, and to rely heavily on this persecuted minority which had to practise its faith in secret, to know how to shelter its priests from the ever-watchful

'A tall black man upwards of two yards high'

45

The house of Boscobel, where Charles
was given shelter after the Battle of Worcester.
This painting, commissioned by Charles
at his Restoration, shows a band of
soldiers approaching Boscobel in
search of the Prince.

46

47

Cromwellian soldiers, and to master the escape routes. The Penderells lived and worked in the secluded neighbourhood of Whiteladies in Shropshire, the country house to which one of his companions guided him, hungry and exhausted after his night's ride. And it was at the Penderells' suggestion that he passed the first day of his flight in Boscobel Wood in pouring rain, while all about him soldiers beat the thickets looking for escapees from the battle. At night, with Richard Penderell, he set out towards the Severn, hoping for a crossing, and got the first of a hundred frights when they were chased by a miller who was roused by the noise. Later the King recalled: 'So we fell a-running, both of us, up the lane as long as we could run, it being very deep and very dirty.' At last they could run no further, and threw themselves to the ground listening for pursuing footsteps. None came; they were not to know, as Richard learned afterwards, that the miller was himself sheltering Royalist fugitives and was in no position to summon the Roundheads. When they resumed their journey it was only to discover that the Severn was so heavily guarded that there was nothing for it but to turn back, and, at the same mill-stream where they had been scared the night before, Richard's courage failed him, for the stream was swift and he could not swim. 'So', said the King, 'I told him that the river being but a little one, I would undertake to help him over', and assisted his companion back to the Penderells' house. There they found another Royalist refugee, Major Careless, who was shocked at the appearance and condition of the King. It was too dangerous to spend the day in the house, so Careless and the King took bread, cheese and beer to a large oak tree where Charles slept soundly on his friend's arm while below them soldiers beat the bushes. As the soldiers got closer, Major Careless, whose arm had become so uncomfortable as to be useless, was frightened in case Charles should move suddenly and fall out of the tree, so he took his courage in his remaining hand and woke the King, terrified in case he should cry out, and together they watched the activities of their pursuers.

At nightfall, now with Humphrey Penderell as a guide, Charles moved on to the home of Colonel Whitgreaves where Lord Wilmot had found a temporary sanctuary. There he found another willing helper, a Roman Catholic priest, Father John

OPPOSITE The adventures of Charles following his defeat at Worcester. The battle is depicted top left; top right, Charles and Major Careless are shown hiding in an oak tree in Boscobel Wood, while Cromwell's men search for them; below left, Charles and Jane Lane riding to Bristol with Lord Wilmot. Charles is dressed as Jane's servant, Will Jackson; bottom right, Charles eventually found a boat at Brighton whose captain was prepared to ship him to France.

Worcester

I goe to find the King

Mr Iane Lane and King :

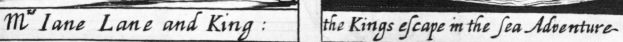

the Kings escape in the sea Adventure

Huddlestone. Together they held a conference, and it was decided that Charles should go at once to the household of Colonel Lane, another faithful Royalist. The Colonel had a daughter, the attractive and self-possessed Jane Lane, who had a pass for herself and a manservant to travel to Bristol, and the Lanes agreed that the King should become 'Will Jackson', and accompany her as the servant. At Bristol, perhaps, a passage to the Continent might be obtained. It was thus an ill-assorted party which set out on the next stage of the journey, including the fearless Jane, her young sovereign in his disguise, and the noble Wilmot riding ahead to scout for danger. Wilmot was a worry. As the King later said: 'I could never get my Lord Wilmot to put on any disguise, he saying that he should look frightfully in it.'

The road to Bristol was a long one, and each day that passed brought its perils. Once his horse cast a shoe, and 'Mr Jackson' discussed the King's escape with the blacksmith.

> And as I was holding my horse's foot, I asked the smith what news? He told me that there was no news that he knew of, since the good news of the beating of the rogues the Scots. I asked him, whether there was none of the English taken, that joined with the Scots? He answered, that he did not hear that the rogue Charles Stuart was taken; but some of the others, he said, were taken, but not Charles Stuart. I told him, that if that rogue were taken, he deserved to be hanged, more than all the rest, for bringing in the Scots. Upon which he said that I spoke like an honest man, and so we parted.

When they reached Bristol, Charles was horrified to find himself in conversation with a man who had fought in the Royalist army at Worcester.

> I asked him [recounted the King] what kind of man I was. To which he answered by describing exactly both my clothes and my horse; and then looking upon me he told me that the King was at least three fingers taller than I. Upon which, I made what haste I could out of the buttery for fear that he should indeed know me, as being more afraid when I knew he was one of our own soldiers than when I took him for one of the enemy.

It proved impossible to get a boat at Bristol, and so Charles took his leave of Jane and set off to try his luck elsewhere. He went first to Trent House in Somerset, then to Bridport in Dorset and finally to Brighton. Everywhere were copies of the

'Proclamation for the discovery and apprehension of Charles Stuart and other traitors his adherents and abettors'. At Bridport he found the inn full of soldiers, and hastily blundered his way past them. 'They were very angry with me for my rudeness', he recalled. It was not until Brighton was reached that Charles at last found a Captain Tattersall who was willing to accept the fee and the risk of taking the royal refugee across the Channel. Even then, Charles was nervous that the £1,000 reward offered by Parliament might prove too strong a temptation, and 'thinking it convenient not to let him go lest he should be asking advice of his wife or anybody else, we kept him with us in the inn and sat up all night drinking beer and taking tobacco with him'.

When the royal adventurer reached Paris he found the whole city agog to hear his stories which seemed to surpass any fiction, though indeed most of them were fictitious because, not being able to tell the truth for fear of betraying his helpers, Charles made up a whole sequence of wonderful events. He told how he had been to London, and adopted the disguise of a gentle-woman. Everyone was amazed and even La Grande Made-moiselle was moved to reconsider him. But Charles was something of a nine days' wonder, and, as soon as the novelty had worn off, he found himself faced with the bleak realities of his position. He was a King without a kingdom; many of his former supporters had hurried back to make their peace with Cromwell; he had no money and no power to influence events. It was not long before he was writing sadly to Jane Lane, 'I have hitherto deferred writing to you in hope to be able to send you something else besides a letter; and I believe it troubles me more that I cannot yet do it, than it does you, though I do not take you to be in a good condition long to expect it. The truth is my necessities are greater than can be imagined.' And, later on, 'I am very sorry to hear that your father and brother are in prison, but hope it is on no other score than the general clapping up of all persons who wish me well. And I am the more sorry for it, since it hath hindered you from coming along with my sister, that I might have assured you myself how truly I am, your most affectionate friend, *Charles R.*' The King, in fact, was no more able to assist his friends than he was to damage his enemies, and from now on he and his diminishing number of followers would

'The truth is my necessities are greater than can be imagined'

have to make the best of inactivity and poverty and fix their main hopes on what was happening elsewhere.

Charles was not unsuited to the task, plunging into the pleasures and interests which played such a prominent part in his make-up. He danced and sang, and took up again the sequence of love affairs for which he was becoming notorious. Within six months of his return to France one of his lovers was credited as being 'His Majesty's seventeenth mistress abroad'. Not surprisingly it was difficult to keep up the court's morale in such an atmosphere. And the shortage of money was chronic. The exiles were besieged with creditors whenever they emerged into the streets. Hyde was too ashamed of his clothes to go anywhere but to the poorest quarters of Paris. Suppliers of wood stopped granting further credit, and during a freezing winter the royal fires burned low or not at all. The court became a laughing stock and Mazarin, seeing little future in harbouring them, came to terms with Cromwell and sent them out to wander through Europe. Charles quite enjoyed his journeying among the towns of southern Germany: 'We pass our lives as well as people can do that have no more money, for we dance and play as if we had taken the Plate Fleet.' There were the usual scandals, enthusiastically reported back to Cromwell by his spies. 'I think', wrote one, 'I may truly say that greater abominations were never practised among people than at this day at Charles Stuart's court. Fornication, drunkenness and adultery are esteemed no sins amongst them.' One scandal which received more than normal publicity revolved around Lucy, by now showering her favours on so many that even the normally tolerant King would have nothing to do with her. For some obscure reason Hyde and his colleagues thought they would solve the problem by having her and her son shipped to England, where Cromwell took great pleasure in shipping 'Charles Stuart's lady of pleasure and the young heir' back again. She was proving a most unsuitable mother, and matters reached such a point that when Charles sent an emissary to wrest the boy away, an unedifying scene took place when she ran screaming through the Brussels streets, shouting that she would never give him up. But Charles threatened to disown her and the child if she refused, and at length the boy was given to Lord Crofts who brought him up as James Crofts as if he were one

OPPOSITE Portrait attributed to Philippe de Champaigne of Henrietta Maria during her exile in France in the 1650s. She is wearing a locket bearing the portrait of Charles I.

of his own family. Lucy died impoverished and unmourned in 1657, by which time Charles had other children by other Royalist ladies to look after: Charlotte Fitzroy by Betty Killigrew, and Charles Fitzcharles by the beautiful Catherine Pegge.

But if Charles was finding amusements, sterner business was not neglected. Hyde was particularly active. Lessons in statecraft were given to the King, unlikely as it seemed that they would ever be of practical use. Money was scraped together to support optimistic but misguided Royalist plotters. The assassination of Cromwell was a constant theme for discussion, while as an alternative there was the idea that Charles should marry Cromwell's daughter, and reward the Lord Protector with the Governorship of Ireland. Innumerable letters were written, despite high and worrying postal charges. One of them was sent to George Monck, once a Royalist soldier but now holding Scotland for Cromwell. It ran:

> One who believes he knows your nature and inclinations very well assures me that notwithstanding all ill accidents and misfortunes you retain your old affection to me and resolve to express it upon the seasonable opportunity, which is as much as I look for from you. We must all wait patiently for that opportunity, which may be offered sooner than you expect. When it is, let it find you ready and in the mean time have a care to help yourself out of their hands who know the hurt you can do them in a good conjuncture and can never but suspect your affection to be as I am confident it is towards your very affectionate friend, *Charles R.*

The confidence was misplaced, and indeed there was little enough reason to look for anything from so cautious a man as Monck. But it was in these ways that the Royalists busied themselves and kept their spirits up. More substantial were their hopes from the war which broke out between Spain and Cromwell's Protectorate in 1655. Charles left Germany for the Spanish territory of Flanders, and from England and the Continent English Royalists hastened to enlist in the Spanish armies. James Duke of York was summoned from the command he was holding in the French army under the tutelage of the great Turenne to take one under Spain, though he did so very reluctantly at the firm insistence of his brother. But Spain proved no more capable than others who had tried to defeat

ABOVE Henry, Duke of Gloucester, Charles's youngest brother, born in 1639.
LEFT James, Duke of York, Charles's other brother, in a portrait attributed to Charles Wauttier. It shows him as a soldier when he served with the Spanish army at the Battle of the Dunes.

Cromwell in battle, and once again the optimism of the Royalist camp evaporated into its customary hopelessness.

Then, in the autumn of 1658 came news which brought all the Royalists crowding into the churches with thanksgiving. 'The Devil is dead', they told each other exultantly. Oliver Cromwell,

the man who stood between them and their inheritance, had died at the height of his power, and surely now England would summon back its exiled monarch. The flurry of letters and coded messages gained in momentum. In England a clandestine body of supporters, the 'Sealed Knot', planned a rising, while other Royalists plotted a *coup* for 1 August 1659. Charles went to Calais to be close at hand when needed. And there he learned of the fate of his followers: how their disorganised, unco-ordinated attempt had collapsed almost before it had begun. It seemed in that moment as if the English Republic was as entrenched as ever, and that the future held no more for the exiles than had the past.

But this was not the case. Something was happening, and so swiftly that it was difficult to comprehend. The Protectorate, apparently so secure, was in reality dissolving into anarchy. Richard Cromwell, his father's successor, had neither the will nor the ability to hold the balance between the multitude of conflicting forces. Parliament was at odds with the army, and the turbulent nature of the regime had divided them both from the people they governed. Quite suddenly men began to consider the alternative and turn their minds towards the King across the water. As 1659 gave way to the New Year, there was a Royalist tide of feeling running in the land, and it could not be stopped. Samuel Pepys noted in his diary that men no longer drank the King's health in secret, but were doing so openly in the taverns. An English Royalist wrote to Hyde:

> You cannot imagine how all people here are affected with joy at the hope of having a King again. His picture is hung up in many places in the streets, and all that go by stop to look upon it; amongst whom there was one yesterday that said he had seen him lately and that he was not so handsome as that picture, at which the people were so angry that they fell upon the man and beat him soundly; by which you may judge of their inclinations.

Away in the north Monck was wrestling with his conscience. He hated committing himself, but he hated anarchy more. In March he sent an emissary, Sir John Grenville, to Charles's court, putting nothing in writing but trusting solely to word of mouth. Charles was no longer the impetuous youth who had erred so badly in Scotland, and this time he made no mistake.

OPPOSITE George Monck, portrait by Sir Peter Lely. In 1660 he marched on London and arranged for the dissolution of Parliament and for a 'Free Parliament' which voted for the restoration of the monarchy.

59

60

The Declaration of Breda, issued in 1660 by Charles, under the guidance of Edward Hyde. In this he promised a general pardon to his enemies and to uphold the Anglican Church, but to grant liberty to tender consciences.

OVERLEAF Charles with his courtiers walking on Horseguards' Parade. The Palace of Whitehall can be seen in the background.

DIEV·ET·MON·DROIT 1660

64

The secrets were kept, and he waited on the general. He took Monck's advice to remove himself from Spanish dominions, and took up residence in Breda. There hundreds of Royalists swarmed to his court, eager for a sign of favour from the coming man. Among them was a beautiful girl named Barbara Palmer, mistress of the Earl of Chesterfield, full in figure, lovely in complexion, radiant in her youth. Barbara was a Villiers, and therefore a member of one of England's most illustrious families. Her husband, Roger Palmer, was a dutiful if self-effacing Royalist; her father, Lord Grandison, had fought for Charles I in the Civil War and had died of his wounds. She therefore had some claims on the protection of her sovereign, and the King's favours were not withheld.

Meanwhile Monck had made his move, marching from Scotland with the only force in the land capable of restoring order. He still kept his counsels to himself, but his declared intentions to call a 'Free Parliament' left the exultant Royalists in no doubt about the outcome. Under the masterful guidance of Hyde, now elevated to the position of Lord Chancellor, Charles produced a Declaration from Breda to remove any lingering doubts. He pardoned his enemies, promised to uphold the Anglican Church, but to grant 'liberty to tender consciences'; and to leave all difficult questions to the will of Parliament. When the gracious message was read to Monck's Parliament the members were overcome with gratitude. By the spring preparations were in train for the King's return to England. A fleet was despatched to Holland, taking with it a chest containing £50,000 as a gift to the King who could remember nothing but penury. In his excitement Charles emptied all the coins onto his bed and called his brother James and sister Mary to look at the sight. And then, on a perfect May morning, he boarded the flagship of the fleet, *The Naseby*, rechristened *The Royal Charles*, and set sail for the kingdom which had so recently seemed completely beyond his grasp.

OPPOSITE Charles's coat of arms at his Restoration, painted on a wooden panel.

3 The
Promised Land
1660-4

THE SHORT VOYAGE from the Hague to Dover was the happiest the sea-loving monarch ever made. It is easy to picture him, moving affably among his subjects who clustered round to listen spell-bound as he told them stories he would be retelling for the rest of his life: of his time in Scotland; his adventures after Worcester; his wanderings in exile. Scotland had left an indelible impression. One of the emissaries to Holland wrote: 'I wondered to hear him speak of all the passages and things while he was in Scotland with as full a remembrance and exact knowledge as if they had been recently acted, and he had lately come from thence.' On board *The Royal Charles* Samuel Pepys was moved to tears to hear the stories of the miller, the oak tree, the Penderells and Jane Lane. In later years the young Earl of Rochester, Lord Wilmot's son, wondered unkindly how His Majesty could remember his adventures in

RIGHT Miniature, by an unidentified artist, of Charles II. The King's heavy dark features and long black curly hair correspond closely to the written descriptions of the period.

PREVIOUS PAGES The procession of Charles II from the Tower to Westminster for his coronation on 23 April 1661. Painting by Dirck Stoop.

such detail, and not remember that he was repeating them to the same audience.

Charles's homecoming was an occasion to set aside, at least for a time, the bitter memories and disappointments of the past. At Dover, General Monck handed his sheathed sword to the King and the Mayor presented a handsome Bible. Charles, who knew the value of a white lie, assured His Worship that he would treasure the Bible 'above all things in the world'. The royal procession moved on slowly and in triumph from Dover to Canterbury and on to Rochester. Each town was a blaze of decoration: tapestries hung from windows, flags flew from rooftops. Everywhere there were crowds cheering themselves hoarse as if to make amends for their republican aberration.

The King entered London on his thirtieth birthday amid celebrations such as the capital had never known. Evelyn watched it all, writing of the

> . . . triumph of above 20,000 horse and foot, brandishing their swords and shouting with inexpressible joy; the ways strewed with flowers, the bells ringing, the streets hung with tapestry, fountains running with wine, the Mayor, Aldermen and all companies in their liveries, chains of gold and banners: lords and nobles clad in cloth of silver, gold and velvet: the windows and balconies well set with ladies: trumpets, music and myriads of people flocking even so far as from Rochester, so as they were seven hours in passing the city even from two in the afternoon till nine at night. . . . It was the Lord's doing, for such a restoration was never mentioned in any history, ancient or modern, since the return of the Jews from the Babylonian captivity.

At the King's Head tavern the proprietor's wife gave birth in her excitement and the King brought the entire proceedings to a temporary halt as he stopped to greet the latest addition to his kingdom. Then on, past the stately riverside houses of the Strand, to Whitehall where he made a gracious speech, though 'disordered by my journey and with noise still sounding in my ears'. A thanksgiving service in Westminster Abbey was cancelled and instead the King slipped quietly away to spend the first night of his Restoration in the arms of Barbara Palmer. There would be enough serious work tomorrow when he would pick up the reins laid down by his father eleven years before.

What the Restoration meant to the English people can only be measured against the austerities of the regime which had preceded it. We must picture lords and ladies searching out fineries they had laid aside during the years of drabness; imported luxuries reappearing in the shops; society hostesses studying the almost forgotten etiquettes of parties and balls;

70

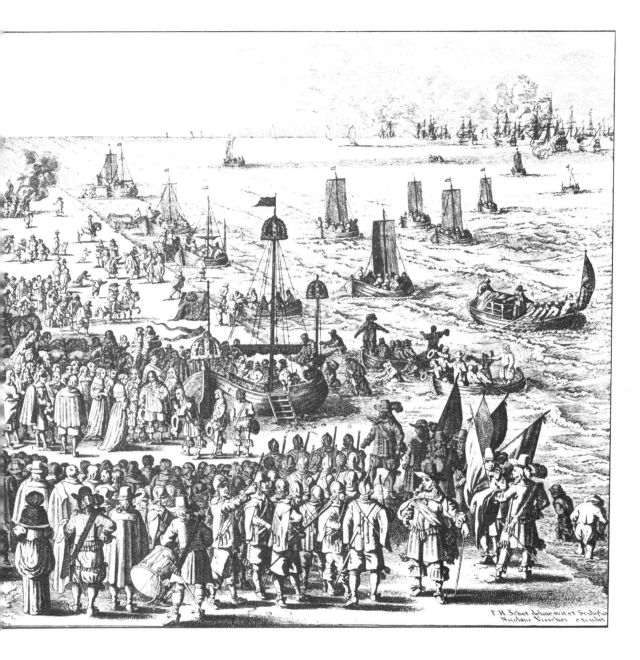

children happy to be able to play those sports and games pro-scribed by the Puritans; composers able to turn their art to other forms than solemn church music; actors and playwrights discovering they were no longer condemned as frivolous and ungodly; church services returning to their former beauty. All these things were very much the concern of the new monarch.

Charles's departure from Schevenigen in Holland to regain his kingdom in May 1660.

71

Under Charles's patronage the theatres flourished. In 1663 he granted a charter (above) to Thomas Killigrew for his theatre in Drury Lane. The second of London's theatres was the Duke of York's in Lincoln's Inn Fields (opposite).

He led fashion, danced, was an enthusiastic sportsman and regular theatregoer. He encouraged his musicians to introduce more gaiety into church services and his churchmen to adopt again the vestments and rituals so abhorrent to the Puritans. Within a short time he licensed two theatres, the King's Theatre at Drury Lane and the Duke of York's at Lincoln's Inn. Under his patronage all the arts flourished; and the sciences too. In August he granted a royal charter to a small group of men who now became known as the Royal Society. One of their earliest investigations led them to place a spider in a circle of unicorn horns to test the validity of the old belief that it would

72

not climb out. Their effort was rewarded when the spider crawled away – one of many experiments by Society members which would, in Charles's reign, culminate in the more enduring work of Isaac Newton.

The new King was well suited to the task of presiding over such a society, and his subjects were only too willing to see in him the fulfilment of all their hopes. Eulogies flooded the presses and the poets vied with each other in the warmth of their tributes. Edmund Waller wrote:

> Faith, law, and piety (that banished train),
> Justice and truth, with you return again.

while Andrew Marvell drew inspiration from the Bible:

> Of a tall stature and of sable hue,
> Much like the son of Kish, that lofty Jew,
> Twelve years complete he suffered in exile
> And kept his Father's Asses all the while.
> At length by wonderful impulse of fate,
> The people call him home to help the state;
> And what is more they send him money too,
> And clothe him all from head to foot anew.

One contemporary enthused more prosaically:

> He is somewhat taller than the middle stature of Englishmen, and so exactly formed, that the most curious eye cannot find one error in his shape. His face is rather grave than severe, which is very much softened whensoever he speaks. His complexion is somewhat dark, but much enlightened by his eyes, which are quick and sparkling. Until he was near twenty years of age, the figure of his face was very lovely; but he is since grown leaner, and now the majesty of his countenance supplies the lines of beauty. His hair, which he hath in great plenty, is of a shining black, not frizzled, but so naturally curling into great rings, that it is a very comely ornament. His motions are so easy and graceful, that they do very much commend his person when he either walks, dances, plays at pall mall, at tennis, or rides the great horse, which are his usual exercises . . . To the gracefulness of his deportment may be joined his easiness of access, his patience in attention, and the gentleness both in the tone and style of his speech . . . Amongst his acquired endowments, these are the most eminent: he understands Spanish and Italian, speaks and writes French correctly; he is well versed in ancient and modern history, hath read divers of the choicest pieces

OPPOSITE In August 1660, Charles granted a royal charter to a group of scientists who called themselves the Royal Society. This illustration shows the engraved frontispiece to Thomas Sprat's *History of the Royal Society of London*, published in 1667. The design was drawn by John Evelyn and engraved by Wenceslaus Hollar.

74

SOCIETATIS PRÆSES   ARTIVM INSTAVRATOR

Evelyn inv DDC   Wenceslaus Hollar f 1667

of the Politic, hath studied some useful parts of the mathematics, as fortification, and the knowledge of the globes; but his chief delight is in navigation, etc.

But even this writer was moved to conclude: 'He is the pattern of patience and piety, the most righteous and justest of Kings; The most knowing and experienced of Princes. The holiest and the best of men. The severest punisher of vice; and the strictest rewarder of virtue. The constantest preserver in religion. And the truest lover of his subjects.'

Such was the acclaim with which Charles was greeted, and his subjects looked forward eagerly to the benefits of his king-ship. Most obvious of all Charles's contributions to national life was the court, centred on the complicated maze of build-ings known as Whitehall Palace. It sprawled for half a mile along the river, the home of the King, his household and his ministers of State. It was to Whitehall that the ambitious flocked, hoping to catch the eye of the King or of the great men

Charles's court was centred on his palace of Whitehall. The palace had been built by Henry VIII, but Charles I had planned to replace the sprawling Tudor buildings by a modern palace to the designs of Inigo Jones. Of this project only the Banqueting House was completed, and can be seen in this etching by Hollar, dominating the lower sixteenth-century buildings around it.

who attended him. It was here that many of the King's public duties were performed, including the ancient King's Touch for scrofula. At these ceremonies the diseased subjects would file past, kneeling for Charles to place his hands on their faces, and to hear him recommend that they go home and have a good wash. Sometimes as many as six hundred came for their cure in a single session, and his reputation was such that he even had an occasional patient from the New World.

The life of a seventeenth-century monarch was a very public affair. Whitehall was permanently thronged with eager spectators: 'like a fair all day' wrote one exuberant Cavalier. When the King dined at midday in the great Banqueting Hall he did so under the gaze of the hundreds who passed to and fro in the galleries above. His officials competed for the privileges of attending even his most private moments. When he slept custom demanded that a gentleman of the Bedchamber lie with him. But Charles never succumbed to the absurd lengths of the French court, once remarking that his royal cousin, Louis XIV,

The Manner of His Majesties Curing the Disease,
CALLED THE
KINGS-EVIL.

London Printed for Dorman Newman at the Kings Armes in the Poultry &.   F. H. van Houe Sculp:

THE Ministers of the Kings Majesties Chappel reading the Common-Prayers and Liturgy allowed in the Church of *England*, when the Ordinary Prayers with the Epistle and Gospel is ended, the diseased persons are brought by the Kings Chyrurgeons into His Majesties presence, where by Faith and fervent Prayer they desire help. Then is read this Gospel next following; and when these words are read, *viz. They shall lay their hands, &c.* The King layeth both his hands on the diseased persons, and with his bare hands doth stroke them: which being done, the diseased persons stand a little aside. Then the rest of this Gospel is read, *viz. So then when, &c.*

The Gospel written in the xvj of *Mark*.

JESus appeared unto the eleven as they sate at meat, and cast in their teeth their unbelief and hardness of heart, because they believed not them which had seen that he was risen again from the dead. And he said unto them, Go ye into all the world, and preach the Gospel to all creatures: He that believeth and is baptized, shall be saved: but he that believeth not, shall be damned. And these tokens shall follow them that believe: In my Name they shall cast out devils, they shall speak with new tongues, they shall drive away serpents; and if they drink any deadly thing, it shall not hurt them: THEY SHALL LAY THEIR HANDS ON THE SICK, AND THEY SHALL RECOVER. *So then when the Lord had spoken unto them, he was received into heaven, and is on the right hand of God. And they went forth, and preached every where, the Lord working with them, and confirming the word with miracles following.*

Repeat the same as often as the King toucheth the sick person.

Which Gospel being read, then this Gospel next following is also read: And when these words are read, *That light was the true light, &c.* The King ariseth, and the diseased are again brought before him; then he taketh a piece of Gold called an Angel, of the value of 10 shillings, with a hole made therein, and making the sign of the Cross on the diseased place, with Prayer and Blessing, he hangeth the Gold in a Silk-string about the Neck of every diseased person. When the King hath so put an Angel of Gold about the Neck of every one of the diseased persons, then the rest of this Gospel is read, *viz. He was in the world, &c.* The diseased persons standing in the mean time a little aside.

The Gospel written in the first of St. *John*.

IN the beginning was the Word, and the Word was with God, and God was the Word. The same was in the beginning with God. All things were made by it, and without it was made nothing that was made. In it was life, and the life

was the light of men and the light shineth in the darkness, and the darkness comprehended it not. There was sent from God a man, whose name was *John*: the same came as a witness to bear witness of the light, that all men through him might believe. He was not that Light, but was sent to bear witness of the light. THAT LIGHT WAS THE TRUE LIGHT, WHICH LIGHTETH EVERY MAN THAT COMETH INTO THE WORLD. He was in the world, and the world was made by him, and the world knew him not. He came among his own, and his own received him not. But as many as received him, to them gave he power to be made sons of God, even them that believed on his Name, which were born, not of blood, nor of the will of the flesh, nor yet of the will of man, but of God. And the same word became flesh, and dwelt among us, and we saw the glory of it, as the glory of the only begotten Son of the Father, full of grace and truth.

Repeat the same as often as the King putteth the Angel about their necks

This Gospel being ended, then the King with the whole company of the Church upon their knees do pray thus:

LOrd have mercy upon us.   Christ have mercy upon us.   Lord have mercy upon us.
Our Father which art in Heaven, hallowed be thy Name, Thy Kingdom come, Thy will be done in Earth, as it is in Heaven, Give us this day our dayly bread, And forgive us our trespasses, as we forgive them that trespass against us, And lead us not into temptation:
    Answer. But deliver us from evil. Amen.
Minister, O Lord save thy servants.   Answer. Which put their trust in thee.
Min. Send unto them help from above.   Ans. And evermore mightily defend them.
Min. Help us O God our Saviour.   Ans. And for the glory of thy Names sake deliver us, be merciful unto us sinners for thy Names sake.
Min. O Lord hear our prayers.   Ans. And let our cry come unto thee.
ALmighty God, the eternal health of all such as put their trust in thee, hear us we beseech thee on the behalf of these thy servants for whom we call for thy merciful help, that they receiving health, may give thanks to thee in thy holy Church, through *Jesus Christ* our Lord, Amen.

Then the Prayers are concluded with this Blessing, *viz.*

THE peace of God which passeth all understanding, keep your hearts and minds in the knowledge and love of God, and of his Son *Jesus Christ* our Lord: And the blessing of God Almighty, the Father, the Son, and the Holy Ghost, be amongst you, and remain with you always. Amen.

Which being ended, the healed persons depart, first giving thanks to God, and to the Kings Majesty, and congratulating one another for their recovery.

LONDON: Printed for *Dorman Newman*, at the *Kings-Arms* in the *Poultrey*, MDCLXXIX.

LEFT Broadsheet of 1679, engraved by Van Houe, showing Charles II giving the King's Touch for scrofula.

RIGHT Gold 'touchpieces' showing the obverse and reverse designs. They were given to people who had received the King's Touch, so that they could wear them round their necks.

could not use his chamber pot without having someone to hold it. And the English King's resourcefulness allowed for an avenue of escape. His bedchamber led off to the apartments of Will Chiffinch, his trusted secretary, messenger, spy and master of the backstairs. A narrow staircase led from Chiffinch's rooms to the water's edge where there were always two or three boats moored waiting to take the King on some private quest for pleasure unobtainable in the overcrowded palace. But Sunday evenings would usually find him in his apartments, writing to his youngest sister, Henriette, whom he called 'Minette'. She was his favourite, a pretty girl, fourteen years younger than the brother she adored as much as he loved her. Raised a Catholic at her mother's court in France, she became his friend and confidante, and in their correspondence are to be found many of the most intimate and revealing passages in which the King unravelled his private thoughts to someone he knew would respond with sympathy and understanding. Now she was left behind, wife of the unpleasant, homosexual Philip, Duc d'Orléans, Louis XIV's younger brother, and both Minette and Charles fretted at the distance which separated them.

They were briefly reunited in the late autumn when she arrived, together with their mother, to join in the celebrations which surrounded the visit of another sister, Mary, widow of the Prince of Orange. It was a joyful occasion, despite the strange behaviour of brother James. He had contrived to make pregnant the Lord Chancellor's daughter Anne Hyde, and now announced that he proposed to marry her. Her father was distraught at the thought of a commoner marrying so exalted

LEFT Princess Mary, Charles's eldest sister, who married William of Orange.

RIGHT Anne Hyde, daughter of Edward Hyde, who became pregnant by James, Duke of York, in 1660. Anne married James and bore him two daughters – future queens of England – Mary and Anne.

a person, declaring that he would rather have her James's whore than his wife and demanding that she be sent to the Tower. He was not uninfluenced by the wave of hostility focussing, quite unjustifiably, on what appeared to be his own interests in the marriage, and rhymes like the following were soon in circulation:

> Then the Fat Scrivener doth begin to think
> 'Twas time to mix the Royal blood with ink

Henrietta Maria was equally distressed, and James himself had second thoughts. Some of his friends came forward to claim that they had had liaisons with Anne, and that she was quite unsuitable as a wife for the Duke. It was behaviour which disgusted the King. He had little time for the vacillations of his dull-witted, ungracious brother, and firmly insisted that he

honour his obligations. James did so, and, although he was not a faithful husband, Anne soon established a remarkable ascendancy over him in what was to prove, on the whole, a highly successful marriage and one which was to provide England with two Queens. The episode was not allowed to mar the Stuart family reunion, but the celebrations were soon overshadowed by tragedy. Shortly before Christmas Mary was taken ill with smallpox, and Charles was at her bedside as she grew steadily weaker. Already he had lost his youngest brother Henry, Duke of Gloucester, from the same disease. Now Mary's death made the first Christmas of the Restoration a gloomy one at Whitehall.

But the coming of spring found Charles again in his usual good humour. In fine weather he could make better use of his home as a place of recreation. Within the palace walls he had his Privy Gardens, his bowling green and his Physic Garden where he grew herbs for his laboratory. Outside the walls lay St James's

A tennis match, from *Orbis Sensualium Pictus* by Commenius, 1659.

82

One form of the game of pall mall – from which the London street has derived its name. The game resembled a rather energetic form of croquet, and required a considerably longer pitch.

Park where the King supervised work on his canal and populated it with various species of bird. Few days passed without a visit to the tennis court on the park's edge: on 5 October 1660 he told his Lord Chancellor at eight o'clock in the morning 'I am now going to take my usual physic at tennis.' Charles's energy was quite astonishing. No matter how late he went to bed he would rise early, often at five in the morning, for boating on the Thames, walking 'at a large pace' for hours at a stretch in the park, hunting or riding. Once he rode to Hampton Court and back, returning at midnight for a Council meeting. A game at which Charles excelled was pall mall, from which the London street name is derived. It was played with a mallet, with the object of striking a ball through a ring which was hung about six feet from the ground. Waller described the King's celebrated prowess:

> Here a well-polish'd Mall give us the joy
> To see our Prince his matchless force employ;
> He does but touch the flying ball,
> And 'tis already more than half the Mall;
> And such a fury from his arm has got,
> As if from smoking culverin 'twere shot.

83

Somehow all these activities left Charles time for business, though he preferred not to separate it from his pleasures more than he could help. He liked to discuss affairs of State between dances, or on the tennis court. Certainly he found this an improvement on the tedious Council meetings which sometimes drove him to distraction or to sleep. It was the Lord Chancellor's duty to keep the King's mind from wandering on such occasions and notes such as 'I beg your Majesty to hear the debate, it is worth three dinners', tell their own story. At these meetings Charles would often arrive with his dogs, particularly his beloved spaniels which he would fondle and play with, oblivious to the sterner matters under discussion. Dogs were a Stuart family weakness, and one Cavalier, who had the misfortune of being bitten, could not refrain from the complaint: 'God bless your Majesty but God damn your dogs.' In all this Charles was setting a new style of kingship. It was something far more informal than had been known before, or was to be known again.

Nevertheless there were formalities which could not be dispensed with, and October saw a ritual which everyone knew to be inevitable. Those regicides who were still alive or had not fled the country were rounded up and the public was treated to the kind of spectacle it most enjoyed. Pepys was there: 'I went out to Charing Cross, to see Major-General Harrison hanged, drawn and quartered, which was done there, he looking as cheerful as any man could in that condition. He was presently cut down, and his head and heart shown to the people, at which there were great shouts of joy.' Charles was not among those who rejoiced. He had worked hard to confine the victims of revenge as narrowly as possible, and after the first batch of executions passed a note to Hyde across the Council table: 'I must confess that I am weary of hanging, except upon new offences.' The question of further executions should be allowed to sleep, 'for you know that I cannot pardon them'.

The punishment of the surviving regicides did not quite end the exorcising of the ghosts of the past. On the anniversary of Charles I's execution the bodies of the great republicans Cromwell, Ireton and Bradshaw were disinterred from their splendid tombs in Westminster Abbey and hung for all to see at Tyburn before reburial beneath the gallows. Evelyn was a witness, and gave thanks for 'the stupendous and inscrutable judgements of God'.

Even more stupendous was the great event of 1661, the King's coronation, which took place on St George's Day. London was blessed with glorious weather as, in accordance with ancient custom, the magnificently-attired King moved by barge from Whitehall to the Tower on the eve of his crowning. All the capital flocked to the river bank to see him and were up early the following day to seek out the best positions along the coronation route. At four in the morning Pepys installed himself high in the scaffolding at the north end of the Abbey, where 'with a great deal of patience I sat from past four till eleven before the King came in'. It was worth the wait. Pepys was enthralled by the fiddlers in their red vests, the bishops in their cloth of gold copes and the nobility in their Parliament robes: by the 'great shout' which went up when the crown was placed on the King's head; and by the shower of silver flung up and down by the Treasurer of the Household, though Pepys

OVERLEAF The coronation of Charles II on its way to Westminster Abbey, 23 April 1661. James, Duke of York, is represented in the second row, the King in the fourth row, surrounded by his gentlemen pensioners. He is followed by George Monck, created Duke of Albemarle for his part in the Restoration.

The execution of the regicides, 21 October 1660.

85

enting
andy,   The Duke of Aquitaine

Garter principal
King of Arms

The Gentleman Usher
with the Black Rod.

The Lord Mayor
of London

17

Sergants at Armes

18

Suffolk
shal, of

Footmen

Pages

Gentlemen Pension

19

Albemarle Master of the Horse;
leading a Horse of Estate

The Vice-Chamberlaine

Captain of the Pensioners

Captain of the
Guard

Catherine of Braganza,
daughter of the King of
Portugal. She was married
to Charles in May 1662
when she was twenty-three.
Miniature by Samuel
Cooper.

recorded sadly 'but I could not come by any'. After the ceremony Pepys managed to get into Westminster Hall where he witnessed the magnificent banquet and the sight of the King's Champion throwing down the challenge to any who dared question his right to rule. And later that night he wandered in the crowded streets, drinking the King's health over and over again, until at last he could take no more and went to bed, whereupon 'my head began to hum, and I to vomit, and if ever I was foxed it was now'.

The coronation was accompanied by the usual honours list which included the earldom of Clarendon for Lord Chancellor Hyde. A few months earlier another earldom had been found for the pliant young Roger Palmer whose wife Barbara became Lady Castlemaine. The rights to the earldom were vested in the heirs of the lady's body and Pepys, who knew all the gossip, noted 'everyone knows why'. But Charles's mistresses and illegitimate children could not provide the nation with a Queen or the Crown with an heir, and Charles was now deeply engaged in planning his marriage. There was no shortage of candidates, but most were eliminated immediately. The King dismissed all the German princesses with the comment: 'Odd's Fish, they are all dull and foggy!'

Charles's choice fell upon Catherine of Braganza, the twenty-three-year-old daughter of the King of Portugal. Charles had never seen her and knew little about her, although he was pleased with her portrait, remarking, 'that person cannot be unhandsome'. But what really won his heart was the size of her dowry – some £300,000 in cash, the island of Bombay and the port of Tangier, together with valuable trading privileges for English seamen in the New World. When these attributes were listed at a Council meeting Clarendon noted: 'His Majesty seemed very much affected.'

Catherine's arrival was delayed until May 1662, and on the 20th Charles reached Portsmouth for his first glimpse of his new Queen. He had ridden hard that day, and was, perhaps, relieved to find her slightly indisposed. He wrote to Clarendon:

It was happy for the honour of the nation I was not put to the consummation of the marriage last night, for I was so sleepy, by having slept but two hours in my journey, that I was afraid that matters would have gone very sleepily. I can only now give you an account of what I have seen a-bed; which, in short, is; her face is not so exact as to be called a beauty, though her eyes are excellent good, and not anything in her face that in the least can shock one. On the contrary, she has much agreeableness in her looks altogether as ever I saw; and, if I have my skill in physiognomy, which I think I have, she must be as good a woman as ever was born . . . You would much wonder to see how well we are acquainted already.

The couple were married on 21 May, secretly according to Catholic rites for the Queen's sake, and publicly by the Bishop of London. Catherine could speak no English, and her convent upbringing scarcely equipped her for the court of the merry monarch. Her retinue of monks and forbidding-looking ladies caused much amusement to the gay courtiers who surrounded the King. But for her part she was prepared to adore the monarch whose exploits inevitably cast him as a romantic hero who had triumphed over tragedy and won his rightful place. And the King seemed prepared to make the best of the match. After a few days he was again writing to Clarendon: 'I cannot easily tell you how happy I think myself, and must be the worst man living (which I think I am not) if I am not a good husband.'

But it was not long before Charles was demonstrating exactly what his idea of a good husband was. No sooner was the royal couple installed at Hampton Court than the Queen was presented with a list of ladies of the Bedchamber. One name was already familiar to her, for she had been warned about Lady Castlemaine and crossed her name off the list. But Charles was insistent, and so began a quarrel which fascinated the court and brought the Queen to despair. Clarendon tried to intervene on her behalf and got the rebuke: 'Whosoever I find to be my Lady Castlemaine's enemy in this matter, I do promise on my word to be his enemy as long as I live.' In his struggle Charles used a variety of tactics. Once he openly introduced his mistress at court, and when Catherine learnt who it was who had just kissed her hand she fainted. Then Charles began to ignore her, and plunged himself even more vigorously into his other pleasures. He had her Portuguese ladies sent home, and left her an isolated figure, friendless and helpless in her misery. Then, quite suddenly, Catherine gave up the unequal fight and not only accepted Lady Castlemaine but went out of her way to pay her compliments and cultivate her as a friend. She began to compete for the King's affections, cutting her dresses lower and her skirts shorter. Charles responded, and for the rest of the reign domestic harmony prevailed. Charles would still sup nightly with his mistress, but returned unfailingly to his palace at night. In his strange way he grew fond of her, and when in the autumn of 1663 she fell dangerously ill, Charles spent many hours weeping by her bed and doing his best to comfort her. In her delirium she thought she had given birth to a child – evidence, if any were needed, of the anguish she felt at her failure to bear the King an heir. Charles assured her she had delivered two fine sons and a daughter. Each evening, of course, he visited Castlemaine, but his relief was genuine when, after a few days, the crisis passed and Catherine was out of danger.

Castlemaine was undeniably lovely, though quick-tempered and easily offended. Pepys noticed how she looked 'mightily out of humour' when the King rode with his Queen in St James's Park. But he was also a connoisseur of her beauty, his admiration mounting almost to a secret passion. In August 1662 'I glutted myself with looking on her'; two years later we hear of 'Lady Castlemaine whom I do heartily adore'; while the following year he had the best dream

> . . . that ever man dreamt, which was that I had my Lady Castlemaine in my arms; and then dreamt that this couldn't be

Tangier, engraved by Wenceslaus Hollar in 1669. The port was the beginning of the British Empire in Africa, and part of the dowry brought to Charles by Catherine.

91

awake, but that it was only a dream: but that since it was a dream, and that I took so much real pleasure in it, what a happy thing it would be if when we are in our graves (as Shakespeare resembles it) we could dream and dream but such dreams as this, that then we should not need to be so fearful of death.

Yet Castlemaine was not the Queen's only rival in these early years of marriage. In January 1662 young Frances Stewart came to court and at once captured the King's susceptible heart. He went out of his way to win her, organised elaborate balls in her honour and wrote a poem about his love:

I pass all my hours in a shady old grove,
But I live not the day when I see not my love;
I survey every walk now my Phyllis is gone,
And sigh when I think we were there all alone.
 Oh, then 'tis I think there's no Hell
 Like loving too well.

But each shade and each conscious bower when I find
Where I once have been happy and she has been kind;
When I see the print left of her shape on the green,
And imagine the pleasure may yet come again;
 Oh, then 'tis I think that no joys are above
 The pleasures of love.

While alone to myself I repeat all her charms,
She I love may be locked in another man's arms,
She may laugh at my cares, and so false she may be,
To say all the kind things she before said to me!
 Oh then 'tis, oh then, that I think there's no Hell
 Like loving too well.

But when I consider the truth of her heart,
Such an innocent passion, so kind without art,
I fear I have wronged her, and hope she may be
So full of true love to be jealous of me.
 Oh then 'tis I think that no joys are above
 The pleasures of love.

OPPOSITE Barbara Palmer, Charles's reigning mistress at the Restoration, painted by Sir Peter Lely. She was created Countess of Castlemaine, and was a dominant figure at court, until, towards the end of the 1660s, her extravagance and fiery temper alienated her from the King.

But 'La Belle Stewart', as she was known, appreciative of all his attentions as she was, would not surrender her chastity. The whole court discussed the affair and took bets on the result. Some of the King's closest friends – including the Duke of Buckingham and his wife, and Henry Bennet – founded a 'Committee for the

Getting of Mistress Stewart for the King'. Once they arranged a magnificent banquet, hoping that a slightly intoxicated Frances would find further resistance impossible. But the plans were too well-laid; the Queen heard about the feast and was intrigued enough to put in an appearance. Seeing the stricken faces of the committee, Charles, who knew very well why they were so discomforted, could not refrain from bursting into roars of laughter, summoning other guests and turning the whole thing into a highly successful ball.

'The lewdness and beggary of the court . . . will bring all to ruin again'

The loose morals of Charles's court were an unfailing source of public scandal, and as early as August 1661 Pepys was commenting on 'the lewdness and beggary of the court, which I am feared will bring all to ruin again'. The gifts and titles showered on the King's mistresses and illegitimate children were a drain on the royal finances, and if rumour inevitably exaggerated the expense, it was nevertheless a growing area of friction between the court and the kingdom which was still, in the main, composed of sober and god-fearing subjects. Money was indeed the King's greatest problem. The Parliament which had summoned him from exile had to be cajoled into providing even insufficient funds. When the King met his first true Parliament in May 1661 greater things were expected from an assembly so obviously loyal and Cavalier in composition. But the grant of £1,200,000 a year never proved enough to meet the King's ordinary expenses, while even then the taxes only yielded some three-quarters of what was expected. By the autumn of 1663, the King had ordered a general retrenchment in expenditure, pruning the household, sending away many of the casual guests who maintained themselves free of charge at Whitehall, and ordaining that only the King and Queen and the Duke and Duchess of York should be entitled to ten courses at dinner.

But the economies failed, if indeed the King ever meant them seriously. And in other areas too there were signs of differences between the King and the subjects who protested their loyalties so loudly. Just because his appeal was to all factions, it was only to be expected that many would be disappointed. Loyal Cavaliers were aggrieved to find that their properties, which had been confiscated during the Interregnum, would not, after all, be returned to them. And in particular there was the question of religion, for the King's preference for toleration did not suit the Anglican temper of the Lord Chancellor and Parliament. Parliament and the Church were adamant that dissenters, whether Puritan or Catholic, should be penalised. The King did not care much about the former, and protested only feebly about a whole series of acts passed between 1662 and 1665 which made it impossible for them to occupy a significant place in either Church or State. But he did care about the Catholics, and here he was confronted with insurmountable opposition. In 1663 he had to abandon an attempt to grant toleration to dissenters – including, of course, the Catholics – as the price of obtaining supplies from Parliament. The most he could salvage was exemption from religious penalties for those Catholics who had helped him in the escapades after Worcester. To most of them he had already given generous State pensions anyway.

But if his subjects found themselves at odds with the King in some matters, on one at least they were united. England was a great seapower and had a right to rule the waves. Commerce was vital, and trading supremacy in any other hands was unthinkable. Yet across the Narrow Seas the Dutch Republic seemed to be developing just such a position, and the nation looked to Charles, whose prerogatives included the making of war and peace, to redress the balance. In April 1664 the King received a Parliamentary petition demanding action, the members promising to give their lives and fortunes in the cause. It was clear that the King would very soon be leading his newly-won kingdom into war.

4 Fire and Sword
1664-7

PREVIOUS PAGES
The Great Fire of London,
1666, from a
contemporary woodcut.

RIGHT *The Royal Charles*,
from an engraving by Van
de Velde. This was the
flagship which brought
Charles back to England
at his Restoration, and
which was captured and
towed away by the Dutch
after their attack along
the Medway in the
summer of 1667.

WHILE PARLIAMENT WAS PRESSING the King to make war, his subjects were already waging it, unofficially, beyond home waters. The conflict raged everywhere Dutch and English seamen were to be found side by side in competition for the trade which was the life-blood of both nations. The East Indies, the West Indies, the Mediterranean, the coasts of Africa and the eastern seaboard of North America – these were the theatres of a war no less real because it had yet to be declared. In the autumn of 1664 came news of a great English victory in Guinea and the capture of Cape Verde. Pepys recorded that the Dutch 'were beaten quite out of their castles almost', and thought that 'it will make them quite mad'. Charles dismissed the protests of the Dutch ambassador with the comment: 'And pray what is Cape Verde? A stinking place!' and asked 'is this of such importance to make so much fuss about?' He was no more disturbed by the ambassador's threat that the prayers offered for him in Holland would have to cease. And soon he was writing to his sister about a more important conquest: 'You will have heard of our taking of New Amsterdam, which lies just by New England. 'Tis a place of great importance to trade. It did belong to England heretofore, but the Dutch by degrees drove our people out and built a very good town, but we have got the better of it, and 'tis now called New York.'

That autumn the King was to be seen almost daily at his harbours, inspecting his ships and taking a lively interest in every detail of the preparations. His own life-long passion for the sea added to the attractions of the coming trial of strength between the two maritime nations. He took the French ambassador De Cominges to see the launching of a 1,200-ton warship at Sheerness, and was so amused when the Frenchman was seasick that he insisted on a return journey by water, and made him rise at five o'clock the next morning to visit Chatham 'to see six vessels, or rather six war machines, the finest and largest to be seen at sea'.

Charles was not alone in his pride and confidence. His fleet of 109 large and 30 smaller vessels carrying 21,000 men and 4,200 guns represented a nation secure in a tradition of naval supremacy stretching back through Blake to the spacious days of Hawkins and Drake. One English admiral thought 'according to an eye of reason, and if God says amen to it, the Dutch are

100

LEFT Frances Stewart by Sir Peter Lely. Frances was one of the beauties of Charles's court, but she rejected the King's advances for several years. Charles commissioned the goldsmith Jan Roettiers to paint her profile in the role of Britannia, in which guise she has adorned England's coinage to this day (right).

not able to deal with our master the King of England'. It was in belligerent mood that Englishmen heard of the declaration of war in March 1665 and awaited news of the victories which the Lord High Admiral, the Duke of York, would undoubtedly win.

Charles, however, had other things besides the war to think about. With his fleet at sea he saw little point in letting the Dutch interfere with his other pleasures. There was Frances Stewart to pursue, and the King did so diligently. He commissioned the famous Jan Roettiers to paint her classic profile and, in the guise of Britannia, used it to adorn England's coinage. It has continued to do so to this day. There was the new novelty from Italy, the guitar, to wonder at, and Charles wrote anxiously to Minette about the delayed arrival of fashionable silk waistcoats from France. And when on 2 June, the breathless Pepys brought the news that the fleets had engaged off Lowestoft it was to Lady Castlemaine's house that he came running.

All the next day Charles and the rest of London listened to the sound of guns as the fleets moved southwards, and when the guns were stilled the whole country went into a frenzy to hear that the broken remnants of the Dutch fleet were struggling as fast as they could back to their shores. It seemed indeed a famous victory, and one which justified all that England had expected. But the truth was less palatable, and the celebrations could not obscure it for those who, like Pepys, realised that England had entered the war amid a shambles of mismanagement and maladministration. Pepys knew that the sailors themselves were frightened civilians, plucked ruthlessly from the streets by the press-gangs. He saw the luckless men shipped off, to the distress of their women, and,

> Lord! how some poor women did cry; and in my life I never did see such natural expression of passion as I did here in some women's bewailing themselves, and running to every parcel of men that were brought, one after another, to look for their husbands; and wept over every vessel that went off, thinking they might be there, and looking after the ships as far as ever they could by moonlight, that it grieved me in my heart to hear them.

And he had observed how every naval contract placed by the government was an invitation to the profiteers, and once noted sadly: 'I see that it is impossible for the King to have things done as cheap as other men.' As he worked into the small hours on his accounts he was only too aware of the chronic shortage of money; the seamen's wages were always in arrears; ropes rotted on the masts for want of replacements. Parliament, so vocal in its promises, was less forthcoming in fulfilling them. Pepys concocted some exaggerated figures of the navy's expenses: 'But God knows this is only a scare to the Parliament, to make them give the more money.'

These cancers would grow quickly enough, but even as the first victory jubilation died down, a new peril appeared from an unexpected quarter. For 7 June was the hottest day Pepys had ever known, and in Drury Lane he saw a red cross marked on three doors, a sign that the plague had come to London. Soon the crosses were to be seen along whole streets. This most fearful of diseases was making its final appearance in England, and doing so on a truly hideous scale. In the first week there were over a hundred deaths, the next over seven hundred, and by September the piles of corpses were rising by a thousand a day. That summer and autumn London – for the visitation was largely confined to the capital – lived with death. Church bells tolling their requiems clanged in ceaseless discord; the mournful

OPPOSITE The Great Plague, 1665, showing citizens fleeing from London, while those left behind try to keep up with the burial of the dead in communal graves.

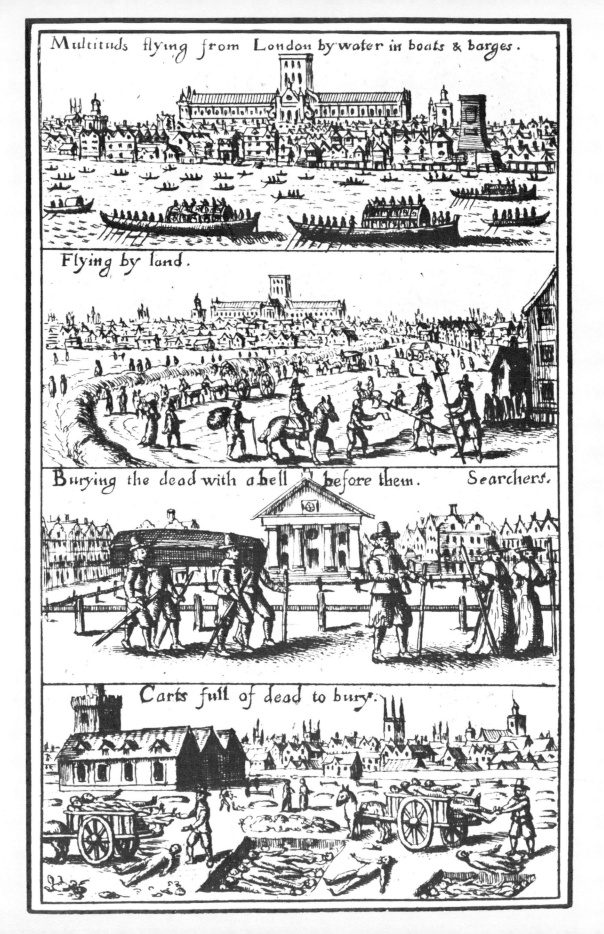

Multituds flying from London by water in boats & barges.

Flying by land.

Burying the dead with a bell before them.   Searchers.

Carts full of dead to bury.

Admiral De Ruyter, the
Dutch commander at the
Four Days' Battle in June
1666. Portrait by Boll.

cry 'bring out your dead' echoed in deserted streets; at night
gangs shovelled the corpses into open graves, drunk out of their
senses in preparation for the revolting task. Inevitably strange
fancies gripped a stricken people: at one time it was thought that
syphilis would prevent the graver disease, and maddened
hordes stormed the brothels in search of such protection. On
another occasion it was rumoured that the plague could be
burned out of the air, and all one sweltering day bonfires blazed
outside every door.

Other localities shut their doors to refugees from London, but those rich enough could, of course, leave for their country estates. People noted how the first to leave included the physicians and the higher clergy. Charles himself was not in such a hurry. As late as 26 July the King was on the Thames, inspecting Greenwich in the company of the young Duke of Monmouth. Pepys was privileged to be on board the royal barge, and noted that Monmouth was 'the most skittish, leaping, gallant, that ever I saw, always in action, vaulting or leaping or clambouring'. But by then the court had left Whitehall for Hampton Court, and soon took up residence at the safer distance of Salisbury. From here Charles paid periodic visits into the remote West Country villages he had last seen as a fugitive after Worcester, and by winter had moved to Oxford to meet Parliament and to spend Christmas. Also in Oxford was Lady Castlemaine, recovering from the birth of her third son by the King.

Charles returned to the capital in February 1666, cheered wildly by those who saw his return as a sign that their suffering was over. But if the winter had killed the plague, it had also brought France into the war as an ally of the Dutch. Charles had spent much time and energy trying to persuade the French not to honour their treaty of alliance with Holland, but in January Louis XIV had finally acknowledged his commitment. In fact he was to give little help to his allies, and the French fleet stayed discreetly distant from the English throughout the remainder of the conflict. But at least the threat was real enough for England to divide the fleet which put to sea in the spring, the main body under George Monck, now Duke of Albemarle, the rest under Prince Rupert to patrol the French coast. On 1 June Albemarle made contact with the Dutch under De Ruyter, and once again gunfire could be heard in an anxious London. This time the guns sounded for four days. Albemarle, out-numbered and outgunned, fought doggedly on. On the third day Rupert joined in the carnage, the English fleet then number-ing fifty-eight to their enemy's seventy-two. Amid the crash of rigging, the splintering of wood and the cries of the wounded, the fleets of the two nations were steadily smashing each other to pieces; and when they drew apart it was only because neither had the strength nor the ammunition to continue any longer.

OVERLEAF The Dutch and English ships during the Battle of St James's Day, 25 July 1666, with a list of the English ships and commanders set out below. Engraving by Hollar.

105

Ship	Captain		
Triumph	Robt Clarke	44	272
Lion	Sr Wm Jennings	280	58
Breda	Jas Sanders	180	48
John & Thomas	Levi Green	200	48
Cambridge	John Jeffries	320	64
Bristoll	John Holmes	200	52
Henry	Sr Robt Holmes Rr	490	80
Princesse	Henry Dawes	205	52
Revenge	Tho: Elliot	300	58
Newcastle	Peter Bowin	200	50
Tiger	John Wenman	160	40

Fireships of this Sqadron

Ship	Captain
Abigaile	Tho Wickam
Samuell	Joseph Paine
Bryer	Willm Seally
Lizard	Joseph Harris
Fox	John Elliot
Alepine	Andrew Ball
Charles	John Johnson

The Blew Squadron

Ship	Captain		
George	Ralph Lasells	180	40
Charity Mercht	Wm Partridge	180	48
Happy Returne	Fran Courtney	190	50
Defiance	Jos Kempthorn R	370	64
Providence	Rich James	140	34
Resolution	Willoughby Hannam	300	58
Elizabeth	Charles Talbot	160	40

July 1666 Together with a List of the English Shippe & Capt with their numbers of Men & Gunns:

Ship	Captain	Men	Guns
Rainbow	Jno. Hart	310	56
Golden Phenix	Fran Stewart	200	60
Mary	Will Poole	300	58
Portland	Rich Haddock	180	48
Loyal London	S.r Ier Smith Adl.	600	92
Amity	Will.m French	150	38
Gloucester	Rich. May	280	58
Unity	Tho. Trafford	150	42
Bonadventure	Wm. Hammond	180	48
Yarmouth	Jo: Parker	200	52
Loyall Merchant	Philip Holland	210	50
Guelderee Ruyter	Robt Gilby	180	48
Vanguare	Anthony Langston	320	60
Advice	Cha: O'Brien	180	48
Victory	St Ed Spragg VA	500	80
Reserve	Jo. Thrwhit	180	48
Dreadnought	Robt Mohun	280	58
Sta Maria	Roger Strickland	180	50
Adventure	Benja. Young	150	38

Fireshyps of this Squadron

Ship	Captain
Blesing	Will Maiden
Guift	Jo: Kelsey
Lands Promise	Munthern
Mary	Wm Harvis
Virgin	Will.m Hughs

May it please yo'r Ma'tie:

Wee have had no tyme since we began the fight
with the Hollander to give yo'r ma't: an acc't: till now; And
now the two enclosed papers will give a Relation of the
whole action (as farr as we yet know) both before and after
the Conjunction of yo'r Divided fleet. We shall now only further
acquaint yo'r ma'tie that o'r masts and saylos and rigging are
very much wounded and o'r Ammunition spent very Low
especially in that part of y'r fleet that began the fight first,
and we have many men hurt and killed, wherefore we desire
yo'r ma'tie that there be speedy order for the pressing of more
seamen and that care be taken in providing of fresh supplyes
of masts and saylos and amunition. The Dutch are gone
backe for Holland very glad as we suppose they are quitt of us
and we beleeve yo'r ma'tie will heare that they have sustyned
great losse in theyr seamen there being many slayne sunke
and Burnt, Seven ships were Burnt and two sunke that we
know of, And from 83 Ships which was the number they
brought to y'r first engagem't: we could not number above 40.
sayle last night when they Left us; But we were also our
selves so lamed in o'r masts saylos and rigging that neyther the R.
James nor the R. Charles were able to follow them, nor so tacke
without repairing

May it please yo'r Ma'tie:

Yo'r ma'tie most Loyall and obedient Subjects

Rupert
Albemarle

Both sides, naturally, claimed a victory, but the ships struggling into harbour and the wounded men they disgorged told a truer story of English suffering and the damage to her fleet. And as if this were not enough, late summer held a still crueller fate for the capital which had seen more than its share of recent sorrow. The Great Fire of London began among the wooden houses of Pudding Lane, and, fanned by a gale, was soon devouring the tinder-dry houses of adjoining streets. Looking out of his window in the early hours of Sunday, 2 September, Pepys could see the glow over the City from his house in Seething Lane. Quite unimpressed he went to bed, but was startled on waking to see the blaze still raging. Hurrying to the City he found a scene of total confusion and the fire out of control, and raced back to Whitehall to bring the news to the King.

All Monday the fire raged, and on Tuesday morning the King and his brother James rode on horseback towards the furnace. They passed streams of refugees, carrying with them what belongings they had managed to salvage. Hundreds more were becoming homeless by the hour. That day the King passed up and down the front line of the fire, scattering silver, encouraging the workmen to demolish houses in the path of the flames, taking shovel and bucket in his own hands. But there was little even a King could do. As fast as a gap was created it was vaulted by the flames. Cheapside was destroyed; so was Cripplesgate. The pride of old London, St Paul's, became a fiery torch, and thirteen thousand houses were burned to the ground while thousands of homeless set up miserable camp in Moorfields where they were visited and comforted a little by the King. A year later Dryden was to immortalise the part played by Charles in these days:

> Now day appears and with the day the King,
> Whose early care had robbed him of his rest;
> Far off the cracks of falling houses ring
> And shrieks of subjects pierce his tender breast.
>
> Near as he draws, thick harbingers of smoke
> With gloomy pillars cover all the place;
> Whose little intervals of night are broke
> By sparks that drive against his sacred face.

OPPOSITE A letter to Charles II giving an account of the Four Days' Battle, signed by Prince Rupert and George Monck, Duke of Albemarle.

THAMESIS

ABOVE Visscher's engraving of London as it was before the Great Fire of London. Old St Paul's can be seen just left of centre. Its spire was destroyed by lightning during Elizabeth's reign, giving it an unfinished appearance. London Bridge is right of centre. RIGHT London on fire, from an engraving by Visscher after Schut. The fire began on 2 September 1666 and continued for six days, destroying much of the City, including old St Paul's.

It was not until Thursday that the wind slackened, and the fire at last died down, leaving behind a rubble which Pepys noted still smouldered in January. Miraculously not a life had been lost; and there were other things to be thankful for, though it would have been expecting too much for them to have been appreciated at the time. There was indeed much that was attractive about old London, still in essence the walled city of the Middle Ages, though now with suburbs spreading beyond, over the fields. Such developments had not gone far: Kensington, Hampstead and Islington were still country villages, while even within the walls urban life was seldom entirely divorced from rural occupations. The centre of London was the City, and it was here that the coalmen, milkmaids, tinkers, mousetrap men and a score of others hawked their goods along the cobbled streets, crying 'Cherry ripe', 'Fine strawberries', or whatever was appropriate to attract the busy citizens to their wares. The noise was unceasing, continuing even into the small hours as the watchmen called, 'Past one o'clock on a cold, frosty, windy morning'. The shops were small and most displayed their signs, such as that outside Mr Farr's shop, 'The Best Tobacco by Farr', or, a little further away, that of his rival, 'Far Better Tobacco than the Best Tobacco by Farr'.

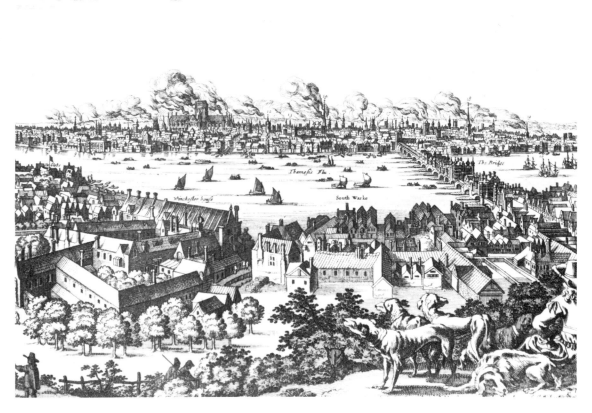

III

For worship the Londoner had his choice of many scores of churches, while for relaxation there was an even greater selection of taverns and public houses. *The Sun* in Fish Street and *The Dolphin* in Seething Lane were among the more fashionable, while *The Boatswain* in Wapping was one of the humbler ale-houses. When he was not praying, eating, drinking, sleeping or working, the Londoner could go to the theatre, or enjoy the more earthy pleasures of the bear garden or the cock pit. Pepys attended a cock fight:

> After dinner . . . directed by sight of bills upon the walls, I did go to Shoe Lane to see a cock-fighting at a new pit there . . . but Lord, to see the strange variety of people, from Parliamentmen to the poorest prentices, bakers, butchers, brewers, draymen and what not; and all these fellows one with another in swearing, cursing and betting. I soon had enough of it, and yet I would not but have seen it once, it being strange to observe the nature of these poor creatures, how they will fight till they drop down dead upon the table, and strike after they are ready to give up the ghost, not offering to run away when they are weary or wounded past doing further, where-as a dunghill brood . . . will, after a sharp stroke that pricks him, run off the stage, and they wring his neck off without more ado, whereas the other they preserve, though both eyes be out, for breed only of a true cock of the game.

And for more elegant amusement there was the wooded beauty of Vauxhall, where one went, by water of course, to enjoy, like Pepys, 'here fiddles and there a harp, and here a Jew's trump, and here laughing, and there fine people walking'.

Bustling, picturesque, even exciting – and yet old London was a relic of a past age. Its dwellings were wooden and dangerous, reaching out across the narrow passages which served as streets, as overhanging storeys had been added in succeeding generations. The streets were unlit and footpads lurked only too frequently in the passageways. In wet weather the passages became open sewers; there were no public lava-tories and Mrs Pepys 'there in a corner did her business' in Lincoln's Inn Walk. The backyard industries of the brewers, soap-boilers and dyers polluted the air and Evelyn com-plained of the 'horrid smoke which obscures our churches and makes our palaces look old, which fouls our clothes and cor-rupts the waters'.

RIGHT ABOVE
The Great Fire, as painted in 1666 by Jan Wyck. In the foreground can be seen citizens fleeing by boat from the City, with all their belongings.
BELOW The entrance to the Fleet River with Bridewell and Blackfriars. This painting shows very well the new type of buildings erected after the Fire. Special regulations were drawn up to ensure that buildings were built of brick and stone with adequate provisions for draught and chimneys to prevent a recurrence of the Great Fire.

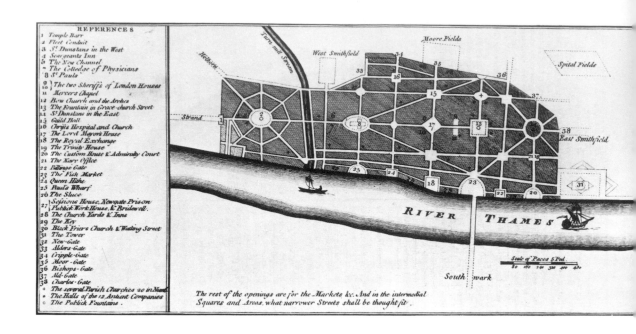

Many plans were made
after the Fire for the
rebuilding of the City on a
grand and magnificent
scale.

RIGHT Sir Christopher
Wren was appointed one of
the surveyors for the
rebuilding of London
after the Great Fire. He
submitted his plan based on
a series of wide straight
streets radiating from
central points. Although
it received royal approval,
this plan was never
implemented.
ABOVE Sir John Evelyn
also prepared a scheme of
his own, much simpler
than Wren's, but which
proved equally impractical.

The capital, in short, had outgrown itself and the fire which destroyed the City known to Chaucer and to Shakespeare allowed a cleaner, healthier, and more attractive London to rise from the ashes. The new capital was not, of course, all it could have been, and was very different from the well-planned city of wide boulevards and stately stone buildings discussed so enthusiastically by the King and Christopher Wren and John Evelyn. Nor had much progress in the rebuilding been made even by the end of the reign. But at least the new skyline had emerged, dominated by the church spires which will always be linked with the man Charles appointed as 'Surveyor-General and Principal Architect for rebuilding the whole city, the Cathedral Church of St Paul and all the principal churches, with other structures' – Sir Christopher Wren.

The Plague, the Fire, the bitter stalemate at sea, the collapse

of revenue – all these made peace a necessity, and negotiations were begun in the autumn. But Charles was not in any hurry, hoping by diplomacy to detach the French from their alliance and perhaps to win by negotiation what he had failed to win in battle. The peacemakers were still arguing when, in the summer of 1667 the Dutch again put to sea, and, in an exploit which rivalled that of Drake at Cadiz eighty years before, broke past the chain in the Medway and reached Chatham. Ranging the land with their guns, and terrifying the inhabitants of the Medway towns, they sailed back into the open sea towing behind them the pride of the English fleet, the flagship *The Royal Charles*. It was a disgrace such as England had never known, and the fact that a peace – acknowledging victory to neither side – was hurriedly concluded a month later was witness to its impact.

Added to this public humiliation Charles had suffered a more personal one. Frances Stewart, so long wooed but not won by her ardent King, had married the unprepossessing Duke of Richmond, a match which astounded the monarch. His anger startled the court. For months he would not receive them, and wrote to his sister:

> You may think me ill-natured, but if you consider how hard a thing 'tis to swallow an injury done by a person I had so much tenderness for, you will in some degree excuse the resentment I use towards her; you know my good nature enough to believe that I could not be so severe if I had not great provocation, and I assure you her carriage towards me has been as bad as breach of friendship and faith can make it, therefore I hope you will pardon me if I cannot so soon forget an injury which went so near my heart.

Then, quite suddenly, the King's anger evaporated. The Duke and Duchess were summoned back to court and installed at Somerset House. They attended balls at court, and the gossips were convinced that the favours Frances had denied Charles while she was unmarried were now given to him when she was a wife. The King explained to Minette that the change in his attitude should not surprise her. 'If you', he wrote, 'were as well acquainted with a little fantastical gentleman called Cupid as I am, you would neither wonder, nor take ill, any sudden changes which do happen in the affairs of his conducting.' Once, Pepys reported that Charles had been seen

OPPOSITE Henrietta d'Orléans, Charles's youngest and favourite sister, from a portrait after P. Mignard, painted in about 1665. Fourteen years younger than Charles, she remained his closest confidante until her tragic death in 1670.

The King's greatest architect

In 1660 Sir Christopher Wren was a noted mathematician – Professor of Astronomy at Gresham College and Savilian Professor of Astronomy at Oxford. The Great Fire of London brought him fame as an architect when he was created 'Surveyor-General and Principal architect for rebuilding the whole city, the Cathedral Church of St Paul and all the principal churches'. He rebuilt the cathedral of St Paul's and most of the City churches He went on to become Surveyor of the King's Works and to carry out work at Hampton Court, Greenwich, Winchester and Kew, as well as to design the Hospital at Chelsea.

ABOVE The Sheldonian Theatre, Oxford, from an engraving in Loggan's *Oxonia Illustrata*. The Sheldonian was one of Wren's earliest designs and was executed in about 1663. Wren attempted to design a D-shaped building without any form of internal support – an interesting problem for a mathematician.

RIGHT The tower of St Mary-le-Bow, Cheapside, one of the many City churches rebuilt by Wren after the Fire.

RIGHT An isometric view of the dome and crossing of St Paul's Cathedral – Wren's greatest work, which was still incomplete at his death in 1723.

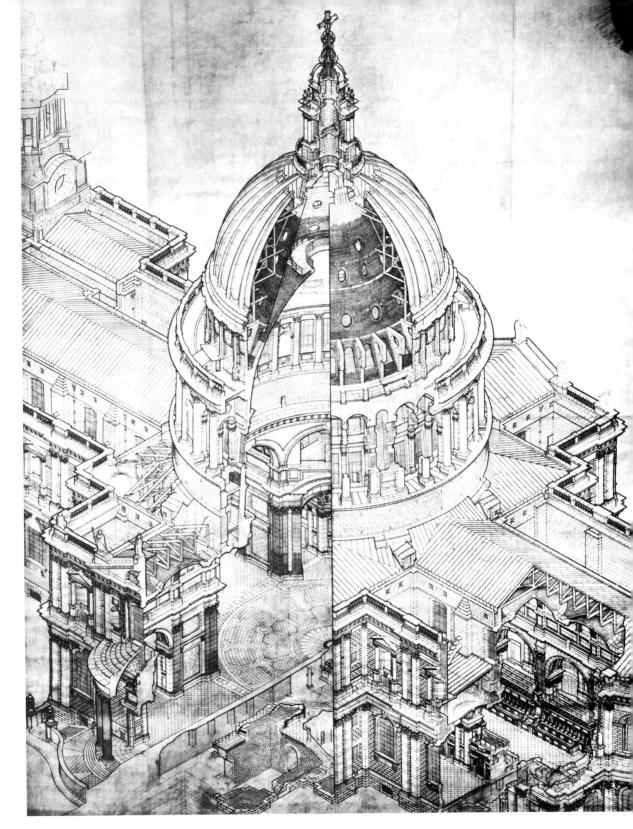

clambering back over the garden wall of Somerset House in the early hours of the morning and righteously recorded 'which is a horrid shame'.

The court which received back the ducal pair had suffered the loss of one great figure. In the anguish of defeat there was not far to look for a scapegoat. The ageing Clarendon had never been popular at court. The King was irritated by his domineering manner, and courtiers like Buckingham and the disreputable Bab May, whose talents were confined to tennis, drinking and debauchery, hated the puritanical Lord Chancellor who made no secret of his disgust. Clarendon would not allow his wife to receive Lady Castlemaine and constantly upbraided the King for his behaviour. Charles alone stood between him and his enemies, and when the King turned against him he was without a friend of consequence.

As chief minister, it was Clarendon who bore the brunt of the nation's frustrations. He was blamed for the war and for the peace. His magnificent house in Piccadilly was stoned by the mob. Parliament began the process of impeachment, but though Charles at least saved his minister from this fate his mind was made up. He sent Albemarle and then James – Clarendon's own son-in-law – to demand the surrender of the Chancellor's Great Seal. Clarendon refused to listen to anyone but the man from whom he had received his office, and at last the gout-ridden old man, still mourning for the recent death of his wife, was summoned at ten in the morning to receive his dismissal from the King. It was a painful interview, but when he left the expression on his face was enough for the waiting onlookers. Castlemaine was elated. Clarendon wrote: 'The lady, the Lord Babington and Mr May looked together out of her open window with great gaiety and triumph, which all people observed.' Bab May could not restrain himself, flinging his arms around His Majesty's legs and declaring that only now could he call him King of England.

And so Clarendon passed out of Whitehall and within a few months fled the country to escape further humiliations. It was a sorry end to a great career. More than anyone he had guided Charles's fortunes in exile and taught him the business of kingship. It was his skill which had produced the document enabling the King to return as the champion of all factions. He had

presided over the complexities of the Restoration settlement with fairness and tact. Of his personality, the best statement is his own:

> He had ambition enough to keep him from being satisfied with his own condition. He indulged his palate very much. He had a fancy sharp and luxuriant, but so carefully cultivated and strictly guarded that he never was heard to speak a loose or profane word. He was in his nature inclined to pride and passion and to a humour between wrangling and disputing, very troublesome, which good company in a short time so much reformed and mastered that no man was more affable and courteous to all kinds of persons.

And he spoke no more than the truth when he added: 'His integrity was ever without blemish, and believed to be above temptation.'

OPPOSITE Catherine of Braganza in a portrait painted by Dirck Stoop in about 1660. She is shown wearing the formal dress of the Portuguese court.

In exile Clarendon lived on for a further seven years, to write his *Autobiography* and to complete his immortal *History of the Rebellion*, arguably the finest piece of historical writing in the English language.

5
High Noon
1667-72

THE COURT WITHOUT CLARENDON was like Hamlet without the ghost. For his part Charles was only too pleased to be rid of the prompting, censorious presence which had always been at hand to remind him of his duties, and the years following the Chancellor's fall represent the high noon of the Restoration monarchy. It was in these years that so much of the King of popular memory – the racegoer among his jockeys at Newmarket, the companion of Nell Gwynne, the 'Old Rowley' of the scandal sheets – established his reputation for posterity.

It was in 1669 that Charles began his regular pilgrimages to Newmarket, making it his spiritual home and horseracing the sport of kings. Every spring and autumn the King would leave his burdens of State behind him and, accompanied by ministers and mistresses alike, would 'put off Majesty' in the way he liked best. He commissioned Christopher Wren to build him a house in the village, opposite the Maiden's Inn. In the stables his Arab horses were carefully tended, feeding on a concoction of soaked bread and fresh eggs. He delighted in the company of his jockeys, and was himself no mean performer in the saddle. Once, in 1675, he managed to win the coveted 'Twelve-Stone Plate'; but, win or lose, his bi-annual expeditions were high points in the King's calendar.

Whether at Newmarket or Whitehall, Charles presided genially over his easy-going court, quite impervious to the stories which circulated freely by word of mouth or in the ever-popular broadsheets. Many of them were, of course, pure fiction; but the exploits of the King and the glittering array of wits and debauchees who surrounded him were as bizarre as anything which could be invented. The Duke of Buckingham, infinitely proud and infinitely unreliable, was an unfailing target for the scandalmongers. He achieved more than his usual notoriety when he killed the Earl of Shrewsbury in a duel, fought because the Earl objected to the attentions Buckingham was paying to his wife. Lady Shrewsbury was herself no innocent, and when the Duke brought her home, Buckingham's long-suffering wife not surprisingly refused to share a roof with such a disreputable woman. It was a reaction for which the Duke was prepared: 'Why so I thought Madame' was his icy response, 'And I have ordered your coach to take you to your mother.'

OPPOSITE Three of Charles's favourite mistresses.
ABOVE RIGHT Louise de Kéroualle, Duchess of Portsmouth, by Henri Gascar.
ABOVE LEFT Barbara Palmer, Duchess of Cleveland, with her first child by Charles, depicted in a miniature by Nicholas Dixon
BELOW Nell Gwynne by Sir Peter Lely.

PREVIOUS PAGES *One last race at Datchet* by Barlow. Charles is shown in the royal box with Windsor Castle in the background.

129

The affair only ended some four years later when Buckingham's peers in the House of Lords ordered him to cease 'conversing or cohabiting' with his mistress and ordered them to 'enter into security to the King's Majesty in the sum of ten thousand pounds for that purpose'.

Another of the King's red-blooded companions was the mercurial Earl of Rochester, best remembered for the epitaph he composed for the King:

> Here lies our Sovereign Lord the King
> Whose word no man relies on,
> Who never said a foolish thing
> And never did a wise one.

To contemporaries, Rochester had other claims to fame. One of his amusements was to play the part of a fortune teller in which capacity he showed a quite uncanny knowledge of the numerous affairs and seductions taking place at court. His secret was a simple one: his spy was disguised as a sentry and stationed by the apartments of the maids-of-honour, dutifully relaying the comings and goings to his master.

And so the stories and scandals multiplied; at one time it was the fashionable Lord Buckhurst spending a night in jail with Sir Charles Sedley, courtier and playwright, for appearing naked in the London streets; at another it was Charles himself, stripped and robbed in the dingiest of Newmarket brothels and only saving himself from a worse fate by revealing his identity. The King's eldest son, the Duke of Monmouth, played his part. In the company of two other dukes, he killed a beadle who took exception to their riotous merrymaking, and Charles felt obliged to grant 'A gracious pardon unto our dear son James, Duke of Monmouth, of all Murders, Homicides and Felonies whatsoever at any time before the 28th day of February last past, committed either by himself alone, or together with any other person or persons'.

But Charles rarely minded the scandals, and indeed he enjoyed most of them, even when he was the central figure. He knew all about his nickname 'Old Rowley', taken from one of the stallions in the royal stud. Old Rowley's exploits were commemorated in a score of verses and ballads, and Charles on one occasion overheard one of them sung by a maid-of-

OPPOSITE John Wilmot, second Earl of Rochester, painted in about 1670 by Huysmans. Rochester was one of the intellectual wits who enriched the court of the Merry Monarch.

honour in her apartment. The King could not allow the occasion to pass and knocked on the door. 'Who's there?' asked the startled girl. 'Old Rowley himself, madam, at your service', replied the King as he put his head round the door.

By this time Old Rowley had made additions to his own stable. He first met the actresses Nell Gwynne and Moll Davies at Tunbridge Wells in 1668 where the court had retired in the hope that the waters would help Queen Catherine to produce the heir she was beginning to despair of. Soon Moll became his mistress, though she was quickly pensioned off. But Nelly was different. Sometime in the autumn of that year she was 'sent for' by the King, and while the event was to deprive the theatre of one of its most talented performers it was to begin for Charles a relationship which lasted until his death. Other mistresses came and went, but Nelly remained, her combination of wit, charm, vivacity and coarseness alternately enchanting and shocking even Charles's tolerant court. Nelly's origins were of the humblest kind, graduating from bawdy houses where she served drinks to the customers to Drury Lane where she sold oranges to the theatregoers. By the time she attracted the King's attention she was established as one of the leading actresses of the day; especially in the comedy roles so much admired by Pepys, who wrote of her Florimel in Dryden's *Maiden Queen*: 'But so great a performance of a comical part was never in the world before as Nell do this, both as a mad girl, then most and best of all when she comes in like a young gallant; and hath the motions and carriage of a spark the most that ever I saw any man have. It makes me, I confess, admire her.'

Despite the august nature of her new position – and the £4,000 a year and freehold property in Pall Mall that went with it – Nelly never adopted airs and graces foreign to her character. She delighted the King by the nicknames she coined for his courtiers. 'Dismal Jimmy' was her name for the Duke of York. She remained unspoiled, undemanding and completely faithful to her royal lover. She called him 'My Charles the Third' because she had had two previous lovers, both called Charles, and was quite open about the relationship. 'Charles, I hope I shall have your company at night, shall I not?' she would call out. One of her few material requests was made, in character-istic fashion, on behalf of the son she bore the King, and whom

OPPOSITE Actress Moll Davies. She was, for a short time, Charles's mistress but was soon eclipsed by Nell Gwynne.

ABOVE Charles, sixth
Earl of Dorset, who was
Nell Gwynne's lover
before she met the King.
He was thus one of the
reasons why she
referred to the King as
'my Charles the Third'.
LEFT Nell Gwynne, the
most celebrated of all
Charles's mistresses.
She is shown in this
engraving after Gascar
with her two sons by the
King – Charles, Duke of
St Albans, and James,
Lord Beauclerk.

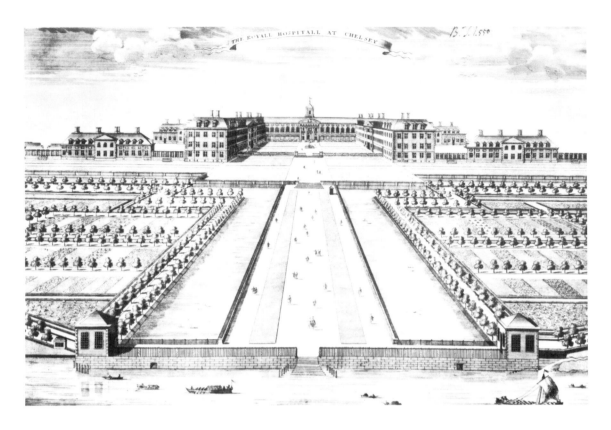

The Royal Hospital at Chelsea, founded by Charles II for his soldiers. Tradition has it that Nell Gwynne persuaded the King to build the hospital. Christopher Wren designed and carried out the building, which was completed in 1692.

she addressed as 'you little bastard'. When Charles remonstrated with her she replied: 'Why, I have nothing else to call him.' A little later the boy became the first Duke of St Albans.

One of Nelly's greatest virtues was that she never sought to interfere in politics at a time when many suspected the King's mistresses of wielding considerable political influence. This was never true, and indeed after Clarendon's fall much of the high policy of the realm was kept secret even from the King's leading councillors. Charles was determined to pursue his political life with the same freedom he allowed himself in his private affairs, and so the Chancellor had no direct successor as chief minister. Instead the King surrounded himself with a group of men of divergent personalities and views who were used at least as much to counterbalance each other as they were used to wield power in the State. The most important were Lord Clifford, a genial pro-Catholic; Henry Bennet, now Lord Arlington, one of Charles's closest companions whose religious views were as uncertain as the King's own; the inevitable Buckingham who, extraordinarily enough, saw himself as representing the Puritan interest; Lord Ashley, unscrupulous, ambitious and Protestant; and the Duke of Lauderdale who ruled Scotland with an iron hand, and whose suitability for the position may be judged from the fact that next to the viol his most hated musical instrument was the bagpipe. The first letter of their names spelt the word 'cabal' and it is as the Cabal that they have always been known. But a less united and more incompatible group would be hard to imagine, or one which was more regularly deceived by a King whose policies they were nominally supposed to be carrying out. They were tools to be used and discarded as Charles set out to guide his country along paths most congenial to himself.

The new policy involved a diplomatic revolution, namely the closest of alliances, militarily and politically, with France, the most powerful country and most absolute monarchy of the age. The drawback was that such a policy was increasingly unwelcome to Parliament and the nation who were beginning to see the strength of France, not merely as a threat to England's security but as the instrument of the Catholic Church. If Charles was to succeed he would have to manage without the support of his subjects, and the result was a saga of tangled diplomacy, duplicity and intrigue which has few, if any, parallels in English history.

The first minister to be fooled was Arlington. He was allowed to assist in negotiating a treaty of alliance with the Dutch which was directed against France to the extent of pledging hostilities if France did not conclude the highly-successful war she was conducting against Spain. It was welcomed by all those who feared Popery, and when Louis made his peace it was widely regarded in England as a triumph for the new alliance. But no sooner was the treaty signed than Charles wrote to the French King, through the intermediacy of Minette, insisting that his real purpose was a French alliance and looking forward to their co-operation against the Dutch. These were hints Louis was more than willing to take, and soon letters from both monarchs were passing through the enthusiastic agency of Minette. Gradually a Grand Design took shape, one which, had it been made public, would have meant civil war in England. This was not so much because of the French alliance itself, for there were

The Cabal

These five men were the leading ministers of the King during the early 1670s. The first letters of their names are linked to spell 'cabal', but they were in fact a totally disunited group, regularly deceived by Charles, although they were carrying out 'his' policies.

ABOVE LEFT Lord Clifford of Chudleigh, a Roman Catholic supporter of the French alliance.

LEFT Henry Bennet, Earl of Arlington. He had received wounds to his nose during the Civil War and always wore a patch

over it to celebrate his courage in the service of his King.

ABOVE CENTRE Anthony Ashley, first Earl of Shaftesbury, an unscrupulous, ambitious and firmly anti-Catholic Protestant.

ABOVE RIGHT George Villiers, second Duke of Buckingham. Despite the scandals of his private life, he maintained that he represented the Puritan interest.

RIGHT John Maitland, first Duke of Lauderdale, who ruled Scotland with an iron hand.

The Duke and Duchess of
Lauderdale in the gardens
of Ham House, Surrey.
The Jacobean house was
remodelled by them to
create one of the finest
residences of the period.

141

still enough enemies of the Dutch to make even that palatable. What was startling was Charles's undertaking to declare himself a Catholic at a time of his own choosing, and thereby reconcile his country with Rome. It was a gesture which appealed to the Catholic consciences of both Louis and Minette; and in addition to a subsidy of over £200,000 for each year of war with the Dutch, Charles was promised a further £140,000 for the specific purpose of imposing his will on his countrymen by force of arms if necessary.

With this astonishing arrangement made, Charles was left with the problem of his Protestant ministers, and in particular the vainglorious Buckingham. He would know about the alliance soon enough, but he could not be trusted with more important secrets. The solution was an elaborate farce by which Buckingham was allowed to think that the French alliance was his idea, and to negotiate a second secret treaty differing from the true one in that the clauses relating to the King's conversion were omitted. The plan worked. Buckingham was received by the French with every honour, and, swollen with pride, concluded his treaty by the New Year of 1671. Ashley and Lauderdale were among the other signatories to this largely irrelevant document.

Meanwhile Charles, Louis and Minette had already settled the real treaty. Minette laboured earnestly in the cause of bringing her brother back into the Catholic fold, and Louis was anxious enough to send over his court astrologer, Pregnani, to speed the good work. The latter move was not a success because Charles could think of nothing more appropriate than taking the unfortunate man to Newmarket to see how useful the gift of second sight would prove at the races. It failed three times in a row, and Pregnani departed under a cloud back to the French court. But the main work went ahead, and in May 1670 Minette arrived at Dover bringing the document for signature. Brother and sister were overjoyed to see each other again, and when the time came for Minette to depart a tearful Charles followed her half way across the Channel before leaving her to take the precious piece of paper, carrying the signatures of Clifford and Arlington, two ministers to whom Charles had now disclosed his conversion, to the French King. Minette also took with her a beautiful Breton girl, Louise de Kéroualle, one of her attendants to whom Charles had taken a fancy. Minette explained that Louise could not be left behind because she had a responsibility to the girl's parents.

Within three weeks Minette had died painfully from peritonitis, though rumour had it that she had been poisoned by the jealous Chevalier de Lorraine, her husband's current favourite. Charles's grief was overwhelming, and for a moment it seemed as if the alliance itself might be in jeopardy. Louis hastened to placate his royal cousin, and hit upon the happy idea of despatching Louise to the English court. She arrived as a maid-of-honour to the Queen, Catherine having learned by now to accept such things with good grace, and soon the whole court was following her fortunes with the keenest interest. But things were slow to develop, and the girl's reticence prompted one French resident in England, the cultivated and witty Saint-Everemond, to write words of encouragement to her:

> Happy is the woman who knows how to behave herself discreetly without checking her inclination! For as 'tis scandalous to love beyond moderation, so 'tis a great mortification for a woman to pass her life without one amour. Do not too severely reject temptations, which in this country offer themselves with more modesty than is required, even in a virgin, to hearken to them. Yield, therefore, to the sweets of temptation instead of consulting your pride.

'Happy is the woman who knows how to behave herself discreetly without checking her inclination!'

Whether or not the letter had any effect we shall never know, but in October Louise yielded. It was an important step in Charles's personal life, as indeed it was in the developing French alliance. The court had gone to Euston for the races, and Lady Arlington was deputed to explain to Louise what was expected of her. At the Arlington mansion the matter was brought to a successful conclusion, Evelyn recording the widespread belief that:

> The fair lady was bedded one of these nights and the stocking flung after the manner of a married bride; I acknowledge that she was for the most part in her undress all day, and that there was fondness and toying with that young wanton. It was with confidence believed she was first made a Miss, as they call these unhappy creatures, with solemnity at this time.

On 2 November Louis XIV sent his formal congratulations to

Louise on her attainment to the exalted role of the King's chief mistress.

Charles's other mistresses greeted their rival with a measure of hostility, but Louise, like the aristocrat she was, ignored their insults with disdain. She had much to put up with from Nelly, who made constant fun of Louise's airs of grandeur and made up suitable nicknames for her like 'Squintabella' and 'Weeping Willow'. Once Louise went into mourning for the death of a French nobleman with whom she claimed kinship. Nelly promptly went into mourning for 'the Cham of Tartary', explaining that she was as closely related to him as was Louise to her nobleman. But Louise had less to worry about from the first of the great mistresses, Lady Castlemaine. Charles had been paying her decreasing attention for some years and when Louise arrived she was more or less in her final eclipse. Though still in her twenties she was losing her attractions, and Charles would no longer put up with her rages and her greed. Her behaviour was becoming intolerable: she would appear at the theatre wearing jewels worth £30,000 and at night lose as much at the gaming tables. When he gave her the great Tudor palace of Nonsuch she promptly proceeded to dismantle it and sell the contents. None of this did Charles's popularity any good, for the extravagance of his mistresses was, as ever, a source of complaint among his subjects. Yet Charles did not altogether desert her. He created her Duchess of Cleveland and acknowledged her latest daughter as his own. But he confided to his friends that he was not the father. She was taking other lovers and it was widely believed that the real father was young John Churchill, who was to win renown as the country's greatest soldier in a later reign.

For the moment then, it was Louise and the French alliance in the ascendant, and the main preoccupations were to finance the coming war with the Dutch and to prepare the ground for the announcement of the King's conversion. In October 1670, a substantial grant was raised from Parliament on the grounds that England's navy must be strengthened in view of the growing power of Holland *and* France. Parliament, little suspecting that the Dutch alliance was in danger, let alone already betrayed, voted the money. Throughout the following year the King increased his standing armies as if he was really prepared for a

144

Louise de Kéroualle by Phillipe Vignon. Louise first came to England in 1670 in the suite of Charles's sister, 'Minette', and was returned to the English court by Louis XIV to aid the alliance between France and England. She quickly became Charles's mistress, and remained in favour for the rest of the King's life.

trial of strength within his kingdom. In Scotland Lauderdale raised an army of twenty-two thousand men under conditions which laid down that they were to serve anywhere the King pleased, while in England the army's strength was surreptitiously enlarged to eighteen thousand by such devices as increasing the number of men in a company and the number of companies in a regiment. Shortly after the New Year of 1672 a further sum of money was saved by the 'Stop of the Exchequer' – an expedient amounting to a freezing of debt repayment and of interest due on loans. On 13 March Charles issued a Declaration of Indulgence, granting toleration of Catholics and Dissenters alike, a first step towards his Catholic design. Two days later came the second step, a declaration of war with the Dutch and the opening of a new phase of the reign which was to reopen wounds not to be fully healed until the Stuart monarchy itself had been swept away.

145

LOUYS
En roopt
Rent
Ik heb n
K Zal
En gan

6 Confusion Confounded 1672-8

RAREL, achter na,
...ing, sta, eÿ sta,
...na de Vrede:
...ig zak met gelt,
...dwingen door gewelt,
...puÿn vertreden.

Maar, Koning, zooje mÿ verlaat,
Ik ben dan zonder moet en raat;
Mÿn kusten die staan open.
De RUYTER met sÿn houte paart,
En TROMP daar elk is voor vervaart,
Zal al den bras af loopen.

THE TREATY OF DOVER held its secrets for over a hundred years, but when they were revealed a debate began which has not yet ended. Who were the real victims of the deceit, the King's subjects, his French allies, or was it Charles himself? Did he seriously contemplate a public conversion to Rome backed by French money and force of arms? Could he have been prepared to assist the French to dismember the Dutch Republic and become a mere pensioner of an all-powerful France? Was he attempting something quite different, to use Louis for precisely as long as France was of use to him, intending to withdraw his support the moment it suited him? Or did he simply manœuvre himself into an impossible position by means of promises lightly given and an alliance whose implications he completely failed to foresee?

The answers to these questions lie in the obscurities of Charles's personality, but one thing at least is quite clear. Throughout his life Charles was, in his political and personal relationships alike, an opportunist. He embraced and discarded his policies as he embraced and discarded his mistresses. Always it was the short-term expedient, the attainment of some immediate objective, which was his overriding concern. It was an old habit. He had acknowledged the Presbyterian Covenant and landed himself in a situation he could never in his worst nightmares have envisaged. He had sought toleration for Catholic and Protestant dissenters and found himself accepting proscriptions against the Puritans and a revival of the penal laws against the Catholics. And now he had made the most startling of treaties with the French; but there is no reason to imagine that he was embarking on a master plan with a firmness of purpose which would have been quite out of harmony with what we know of his character and his record.

There was, naturally, a good deal about his new arrangements which seemed attractive enough. On the religious side, Charles had always been well-disposed to the Catholics. His mother, his wife, his sister and chief mistress were all Catholics. He never forgot that it was Catholic families who had saved him after the battle of Worcester. He knew, though his subjects did not yet know, that the Duke of York had been a convert for some two years past and that in the secrecy of his household masses were celebrated each morning by Jesuit priests. This is not to say that

PREVIOUS PAGES Political cartoon showing Charles on horseback, with Louis XIV running after him, trying to buy his support.

148

Charles himself was sincere in his own conversion. In religious matters he was sceptical enough to remark once that the only *visible* Church he knew was Harrow-on-the-Hill. And when Louis arranged for priests to be sent to England to instruct the King in his new faith, Charles caused endless delays by insisting that he wanted a priest who was also a scientist, because there were problems relating to the scientific basis of Catholicism which he needed to discuss. But nevertheless the attractions of the religion were real enough, and were reinforced by more trivial considerations: the desire to please Minette, to dismay the Presbyterians who had so abused him when he was in their power, and his delight in fooling his inflated Protestant ministers who would never suspect him capable of managing such a *coup*.

And, perhaps above all, there was the magnetic pull of France and her great King. The seventeenth century was indeed the age of France as the sixteenth had been that of Spain. French manners, fashions, and literature set the pattern for the rest of Europe to follow. Everything new from sedan chairs to dainty silver brushes for cleaning teeth were French; even drinking tea and coffee were customs imported from France. In his memoirs the Comte de Grammont wrote of how 'Perfumed gloves, pocket looking-glasses, elegant boxes, apricot paste, essences and other small wares of love arrived every week from Paris'. At the centre of French life was Louis in his Palace of Versailles, surrounded by nobles whose ambitions were limited to a scramble for such privileges as helping the King dress and undress. Louis never met a Parliament. His armies were held to be invincible and were the terror of the rest of Europe. His Divine Right to rule was enthusiastically supported by his cardinals, bishops and priests. It is scarcely surprising that his cousin should have wished to move closer to the Sun King, and to bask in something of the warmth which radiated from Versailles.

But however understandable his motives, Charles has been condemned by generations of historians for sacrificing his nation's interests to those of England's traditional enemy. Such a view is quite unrealistic and demands of Charles a notion of patriotism he would not have recognised. It was Englishmen who had killed his father and Frenchmen who had supported

PREVIOUS PAGES
Louis XIV visiting the
tapestry works of Gobelins
with his *surintendant*,
Colbert. Louis was the
greatest king of his epoch,
and the artistic life of his
court set the pattern for the
rest of Europe to follow.

the exiled court. To suggest that he should have shunned the attractions of a French alliance in favour of those constant critics who held and withheld the purse-strings and whose only saving grace was that they were English is asking too much.

Yet whatever high hopes Charles may have had, they were destroyed by the failure of his fleet in his Second Dutch War. His French allies moved from triumph to triumph, sweeping the Dutch back beyond their borders, forcing them to breach the dykes and flood their countryside to stop the onward march. Faced with annihilation the Dutch murdered their leaders, the De Witt brothers, and placed themselves under the control of William, Charles's own nephew and head of the House of Orange. And so began that long and dogged struggle in which William, against seemingly impossible odds, managed somehow to hold the French at bay, while England watched ingloriously from the sidelines. For England enjoyed no victories. No lessons had been learned from the first war. Ships continued to rot through lack of money, lack of effort and the unfailing corruption of officials. In May the fleets met in a bloody but inconclusive battle. The Earl of Sandwich, commanding for England under the Duke of York, lost his life. No English troops could be landed on Dutch territory – certainly there were none of the spectacular triumphs which alone might have strengthened Charles's hand against the Parliament which met in February 1673, seething about a war declared in their absence, a Declaration of Indulgence published without their knowledge, and alarmed by the prospect of French domination of the Low Countries and with it the inevitable triumph of Popery.

It was a crucial moment, and one which was to alter the character and atmosphere of the reign. From now on Charles's preoccupations would be increasingly with the assembled ranks of the Lords and Commons of England, critical of his policies, extravagant in their demands. Their weapons were formidable, for they could refuse the King the supplies he so desperately needed unless he bowed to their wishes. But Charles was not defenceless. For one thing, he alone had the power of life or death over their meetings, for Parliament could be prorogued, or, in the last resort, dissolved and new elections called. Dissolution was not something to contemplate lightly. The present

152

Parliament had served the King since the second year of his Restoration, and for all its criticisms he knew he was unlikely to get a more amenable one. And he had other weapons: the Crown still held resources of patronage, and members could be bribed with money or office to support the royal programme. Above all the business of government was still in the hands of the King and the ministers he alone selected. He could therefore seek to postpone a showdown while he looked for alternatives – money from Louis, for example, who had every reason to help the English King in his efforts to avoid dependence on an institution which was increasingly hostile to France and well-disposed towards the Dutch.

Time had altered the buoyantly Cavalier mood in which Parliament had first assembled, while inevitable by-elections, caused by death and resignation, had brought a large sprinkling of newer members unhampered by old memories and old loyalties. Some of Charles's former friends and colleagues were now in opposition – among them Ashley, now Lord Shaftesbury, and Buckingham. There were many whose implacable hatred of Catholicism had been inflamed by the Declaration of Indulgence, and when Charles met his Parliament it was with a show of bravado he could hardly have felt. 'I will deal plainly with you', he told them, 'I am resolved to stick to my Declaration.' He might as well have remained silent for all the effect his words had. The Commons made it clear to him that in their opinion 'Penal Statutes in matters ecclesiastical cannot be suspended but by Act of Parliament'. They refused to grant supplies until the Declaration was withdrawn, and, just a month after his announcement, Charles was compelled to give way.

But abandoning his Declaration in such humiliating circumstances did not save Charles from an even greater defeat. For Parliament at once moved on to pass a Test Act which required every office holder under the Crown to acknowledge the Anglican Church. It was shrewdly aimed at the Catholics who, it was rightly suspected, were in the employment of the King; and the triumphant members of Parliament watched expectantly to see who would be forced into private life.

They did not have to wait long. Lord Clifford's secret was exposed when the doors of his carriage were accidently flung

'I will deal plainly with you, I am resolved to stick to my Declaration.'

open to reveal the figure of his confessor in priestly dress. He laid down his Treasurer's staff and died shortly afterwards – it was rumoured by his own hand. In the Queen's chambers there was gloom as her Catholic maids-of-honour drew lots to see which of them should depart, for only nine were permitted to remain. When eight had been chosen Catherine stopped the lottery and added the name of the ninth herself – Louise de Kéroualle, recently created Duchess of Portsmouth. It was a remarkable demonstration of her love for her husband, and of the change in their relationship since the stormy scenes of the first months of their marriage.

But the most prominent victim was none other than the Duke of York, heir apparent to the throne. His resignation as Lord High Admiral disclosed his conversion for all to see, and alarmed everyone who feared the prospect of an unending Catholic succession. The fears were increased when James, with a dramatic sense of ill-timing, decided it was time to re-marry. His first wife, who had herself been a strong influence on his own conversion, had been dead for over two years. Now he considered the attractions of two other Catholic candidates, fifteen-year-old Mary of Modena, and her Aunt Leonora, fifteen years older. In the prevailing atmosphere both were equally unsuitable, both wished to becomes nuns, and James was so uncertain that when his proxy, Lord Peterborough, went to France to complete the transaction, the space for the bride's name was left blank on his instructions. Eventually the choice fell on Mary, and she arrived in November to face a hostile reception by citizens firmly convinced by the rumours that she was the Pope's eldest daughter. The Lord Mayor of London declined to welcome her, 'nor would the City be brought to make bonfires'. When Parliament met that autumn the members would do little but debate the perils of the Duke's marriage and pass resolutions against 'Popish Councillors'.

They demanded, unsuccessfully, the dismissal of Arlington, who they held responsible for the French alliance, and of Lauderdale who had raised the spectre of a standing army in Scotland. A series of prorogations did nothing to cool tempers, and in the New Year Charles made a last effort to save his French policy. In a speech to both Houses he used all the arts of flattery and cajolery of which he was, and had to be a master.

> My Lords and Gentlemen [he began], when I parted with you last, it was but for a little time, and with a resolution of meeting suddenly again. That alone was enough to satisfy my friends that they need not fear, and my enemies that they could not hope for, a breach between us. I then told you that the time of this short recess should be employed in doing such things as might add to your satisfaction: I hope I have done my part towards it. And if there be anything else which you think wanting to secure Religion or Propriety, there is nothing which you shall reasonably propose, but I shall be ready to receive it.

'It is not possible', he assured them, 'for me to doubt your affections at any time, much less at such a time as this, when the evidences of your affection are become so necessary to us all.' And finally he reached his main point:

> I cannot conclude without showing the entire confidence I have in you. I know you have heard much of my alliance with France; and I believe it hath been very strangely represented to you, as if there were certain secret Articles of dangerous consequence; but I will make no difficulty of letting the Treaties and all the Articles of them, without any the least reserve, to be seen by a small Committee of both Houses, who may report to you the true scope of them; and I assure you, there is no other Treaty with France, either before or since, not already printed, which shall not be made known.

It was, of course a monstrous lie, for the Dover Treaty was, naturally, not disclosed; and it was observed that when Charles spoke he seemed nervous and fumbled with his notes. But Parliament was not to be placated and no money was forthcoming. In February, in complete defiance of his treaty obligations, Charles brought to an end a war he had no hope of affording, and prorogued the Parliament he had no hope of managing. He also dismissed Shaftesbury, now openly leader of the opposition, from his ministerial post. Shaftesbury's response was ominous: 'It is only laying down my gown and girding my sword.'

'It is only laying down my gown and girding my sword.'

Charles had succeeded in dividing his people to a degree unknown since the Civil War, and out of the turmoil emerged new alignments and new protagonists. For the King, Thomas Osborne, shortly to be created Earl of Danby, entered the lists. He had been introduced at court by the Duke of Buckingham,

LEFT Mary of Modena
by Verelst. Mary married
James, Duke of York in
September 1673. His
choice of a Catholic
princess was extremely
unpopular.
ABOVE James, Duke of
York, from a miniature by
Samuel Cooper.

but soon outstripped his patron in political influence: able, industrious and a brilliant financier, he made himself indispensable by his management of money and men. His loyalty was to the King and to the Anglican Church. For the Catholics and for France he cared not at all. But he was capable of restoring a semblance of order to the King's chaotic finances, assisted fortuitously by an expansion of trade which, temporarily, brought a welcome increase in customs revenue for which Charles was not dependent on Parliament. And, by judicious bribes, he built up a body of support among members of Parliament which could usually be relied on for a majority. Out of his activities was born a Court Party, soon to be called insultingly by their enemies 'Tories', the name given to Irish thieves and rebels.

Opposing him was Shaftesbury, warped in body but agile in mind, who campaigned ceaselessly against the court, against the Duke of York, against the Queen, and on behalf of the Dutch who should, he thought, be helped in their fight against Catholic France. Shaftesbury's strength lay in the City of London, in the mobs which could be mobilised under the 'No Popery' banner, and in the coffee houses where his supporters met to exchange plans and pamphlets. He presided over the Green Ribbon Club whose members flaunted the colours of their allegiance. They were the nucleus of a Country Party opposition he was building against the followers of the court, and they became known derisively as 'Whigs' or Scottish outlaws. He looked for assistance to the Dutch whose agents could be relied upon for bribes; and even to Louis who was an unrelenting enemy of Danby, whom he blamed for England's withdrawal from the war and whom he knew to be hostile to the French interest. Louis was not above bribing the Country Party members against Danby, a strange and twisted alliance which spoke volumes for the political morality of the age. It was even possible for some to collect from Louis, Danby and the Dutch at the same time, and the name 'Pensionary Parliament' bestowed on this quarrelsome assembly was well earned.

It cannot be said that Charles's personal life was greatly affected by these troubles. He continued to play tennis in the mornings, and to dance in the evenings. The spring and autumn meetings at Newmarket were as splendid as ever. The theatre

OPPOSITE Thomas Osborne, Earl of Danby, a portrait from the studio of Lely. Danby emerged as a leading minister following the turmoil of 1673.

flourished and playwrights like Dryden, Etheredge and Sedley wrote the witty, immoral comedies so loved by the King. Even Buckingham wrote a successful satire, *The Rehearsal*, while that remarkable phenomenon, the woman playwright, had emerged in the person of Aphra Behn. So oblivious did the King seem to his more pressing affairs that one city merchant wrote: 'The truth is this year the Government begins to thrive marvellous well, for its eats and sleeps as heartily as I have known it, nor doth it vex and disquiet itself with that foolish, idle, impertinent thing called business.'

But, much as he would have liked, Charles was not allowed to forget his business. Danby's herculean efforts could not keep the monarchy solvent, and 1675 saw two unpleasant Parliamentary sessions, in the spring and in the autumn. Once again the old grievances were raised, and the supplies granted were less than the King's needs. Charles was urged to enforce the penal laws against the Catholics with more vigour and to make war on France. An attempt was even made to impeach Danby. Nothing could be done, and in November Parliament was prorogued for fifteen months, the longest recess Charles had yet given them and the longest respite he had yet been able to give himself. At least he had gained time, and he used it to try to strengthen his position. Opponents like Lord Halifax were dismissed from the Privy Council, while an attempt was made to close those coffee houses where anti-government literature was spread and seditious talk fostered. Shaftesbury was given a broad hint that he could be better occupied out of London and at home in the country – one which was not taken. Meanwhile Charles turned again to his old policy, dragging a reluctant Danby in tow, and reopened negotiations with France in the hope of renewing the subsidy which had lapsed when England had withdrawn from the war.

In this Charles was successful, and in February 1676 a new treaty was made which, since it bound both parties not to treat with each other's enemies, was clearly directed against the Dutch. But the risks were obvious, and Danby was too frightened to put his name to the document which was written and sealed by the King's own hand. The French ambassador pitied a monarch who had no servants in whom he could trust.

It was indeed a difficult game which Charles was playing, and one which was suddenly complicated by a domestic interlude of a kind only too familiar to the King's court. It revolved around Hortense Mancini, youngest of the nieces of Cardinal Mazarin, and at twenty-nine still acclaimed the most beautiful woman of her age. Hers was a romantic story. She had fled from her intolerable husband – a religious maniac who imposed absurd penances on his wife as well as himself – to lead the life of an adventuress which was the gossip of all Europe. And she was known to have a grievance against the French King who had ignored her constant petitions for the return of what was left of the fortune she had brought her husband. Now she had arrived in England, dressed as a man, and in the diplomatic capitals men watched anxiously to see what political changes, if any, would result.

It was not to be expected that Charles would fail to succumb to the charms of this brilliant and exciting woman: nor did he. Louise's enemies were exultant, and noted happily that the new mistress seemed to occupy all the King's attentions. Nelly celebrated the eclipse of her great rival by going into mourning. More seriously, the French ambassador de Courtin urged his government not to underestimate the danger. 'We have the whole kingdom and the chief minister against us here', he warned, and 'if we are to have the mistress too, I leave you to judge of the future.'

But the crisis did not last for long. Others were always inclined to overrate the political influence the King allowed to his mistresses. Moreover Hortense herself was entirely disinterested in such matters, and never sought to participate in the buying and selling of offices and honours so assiduously practised by Louise. Gradually the affair became less intense; the King's visits less frequent. Louise re-established herself at court, and the French faction breathed more easily. The alliance was not threatened, and the subsidy was safely negotiated. But the sum won amid these distractions was only £100,000 a year, nowhere near enough to keep Parliament at bay for much longer.

It met in February 1677, angry at the long recess. Shaftesbury, with Buckingham a willing associate, opened the attack by claiming that the fifteen-month interval automatically amounted to a dissolution and demanding fresh elections. They

'We have the whole kingdom against us here, if we are to have the mistress too, I leave you to judge the future'

DIEV ET MON DROIT

By the King.

A PROCLAMATION
FOR THE
Suppression of Coffee-Houses.

CHARLES R.

Hereas it is most apparent, that the Multitude of Coffee-houses of late years set up and kept within this Kingdom, the Dominion of Wales, and the Town of Berwick upon Tweed, and the great resort of Idle and disaffected persons to them, have produced very evil and dangerous effects; as well for that many Tradesmen and others, do therein mis-spend much of their time, which might and probably would otherwise be imployed in and about their Lawful Callings and Affairs; but also, for that in such Houses, and by occasion of the meetings of such persons therein, divers False, Malitious and Scandalous Reports are devised and spread abroad, to the Defamation of His Majesties Government, and to the Disturbance of the Peace and Quiet of the Realm; His Majesty hath thought it fit and necessary, That the said Coffee-houses be (for the future) Put down and Suppressed, and doth (with the Advice of His Privy Council) by this His Royal Proclamation, Strictly Charge and Command all manner of persons, That they or any of them do not presume from and after the Tenth day of January next ensuing, to keep any Publick Coffee-house, or to Utter or sell by retail, in his, her or their house or houses (to be spent or consumed within the same) any Coffee, Chocolet, Sherbett or Tea, as they will answer the contrary at their utmost perils.

And for the better accomplishment of this his Majesties Royal Pleasure, His Majesty doth hereby Will and require the Justices of Peace within their several Counties, and the Chief Magistrates in all Cities and Towns Corporate, that they do at their next respective General Sessions of the peace (to be holden within their several and respective Counties, Divisions and Precincts) recall and make void all Licenses at any time heretofore Granted, for the selling or Retailing of any Coffee, Chocolet, Sherbett or Tea. And that they or any of them do not (for the future) make or grant any such License or Licenses, to any person or persons whatsoever. And his Majesty doth further hereby declare, that if any person or persons shall take upon them, him or her, after his, her or their License or Licenses recalled, or otherwise without License, to sell by retail (as aforesaid) any of the Liquors aforesaid, that then the person or persons so Offending, shall not only be proceeded against, upon the Statute made in the Fifteenth year of His Majesties Reign (which gives the forfeiture of five pounds for every moneth wherein he, she or they shall offend therein) but shall (in case they persevere to Offend) receive the severest punishments that may by Law be inflicted.

Given at Our Court at Whitehall, this Nine and twentieth day of December 1675. in the Seven and twentieth year of Our Reign.

God save the King.

LONDON,
Printed by the Assigns of John Bill, and Christopher Barker,
Printers to the Kings most Excellent Majesty, 1675.

were confident that their Country Party would triumph in any new appeal to the electorate, but had seriously miscalculated the attitude of their fellow peers. The Lords were as indignant as the King at the impertinence, and both men were despatched unceremoniously to the Tower. The confinement was not a harsh one, and Shaftesbury was permitted to make use of his own cook, claiming that he feared poison. 'You see, my lords, what he thinks of me', the King told his fellow peers. But the punishment at least deprived the opposition of its leaders, and Charles was able to handle the first session with some success. He obtained a large grant, though it was made clear to him that anti-French feeling was running high and that unless he could prevail on William and Louis to make peace he would find the pressure to declare war on France almost irresistible.

ABOVE A water-colour print of a coffee-house in 1668. The coffee-houses were to become meeting places for the supporters of Shaftesbury, opposed to Catholicism, the Queen, the Duke of York and France.

OPPOSITE In December 1675, Charles issued a royal proclamation aimed at suppressing the coffee-houses.

163

PREVIOUS PAGES In 1677
Charles decided he must
cement an alliance with
William, the ruler of
Holland and his own
nephew. He therefore
supported his marriage
to Mary, the fifteen-
year-old daughter of
James, Duke of York. The
marriage appalled the
young bride, a reaction not
reflected in this idealised
apotheosis, painted by
James Thornhill on the
ceiling of the Royal
Hospital at Greenwich.

Moreover there was increasing talk of a particularly dangerous kind, for attention was now focussing on the Duke of York and there were demands that he should be excluded, as a Catholic, from the succession. Buckingham had a different suggestion. He urged the King to have Catherine kidnapped and sent to Virginia, where, after a suitable period, he could divorce her on grounds of desertion, marry a Protestant queen and give the country a Protestant heir. It is doubtful if the idea could have worked. Louise had borne the King his thirteenth and last acknowledged illegitimate child. At about this time he contracted a venereal disease, and it is unlikely that he was now capable of providing an heir. But in any case Charles would not listen to the enemies of his wife or his brother. For his Queen, he declared that he would rather see her killed than put her away, while for the succession he never wavered in his belief in legitimate succession through royal blood.

But he did work hard to try to find some area of compromise between France and the Dutch, though his efforts foundered on Louis's determination not to surrender his conquests, and William's not to accept a peace which would leave his frontiers vulnerable to future French aggression. Some further gesture was needed to conciliate his enemies, and in the autumn of 1677 William himself, the Protestant champion, arrived in England to a hero's welcome from the Shaftesbury faction in London.

His errand was a spectacular one. Charles, prompted by Danby, had decided on his gesture, and the sacrifice was to be the Duke of York's fifteen-year-old daughter Mary. The prospect of marriage to the small, ungainly, serious man to whom she was introduced reduced her to tears; but her wishes in the matter were not consulted. The couple were married on 4 November and when they went to bed that night Charles tried to introduce a note of jollity into the somewhat subdued proceedings, with the advice: 'Now nephew, to your work! Hey! St George for England!' But William was not a jovial soul. He cut a poor figure among the rakes at Charles's court; though he did display one uncharacteristic burst of initiative when, drunk almost to a stupor, he was discovered trying clumsily to break into the bedrooms of the maids-of-honour.

When Louis heard about the marriage he was understandably outraged, and Charles now even went through the motions of threatening war with France, and strengthened his standing army, ostensibly for this purpose. He continued, of course, to try to hedge his bets, explaining to the French that he intended merely to deceive his subjects. Extraordinarily enough Danby even squeezed a further £300,000 out of the French monarch, though his own countrymen were less forthcoming. They suddenly took fright at the thought of their King backed by his standing army, and wondered if they had been tricked. Perhaps the army was to be used not against France but to impose Catholicism by force. Without a sufficient Parliamentary grant Charles had little option but to give way, and his troops were gradually disbanded.

When Parliament was prorogued for the summer the breach between sovereign and subjects was as wide as ever. Men were suspicious of the King's real intentions; alarmed about Popery; worried about a Catholic succession; distrustful of Danby who, they feared, sought to make the King absolute and independent of Parliament. Above all they were afraid of France whose power seemed at its zenith when, in July, peace was at last concluded at Nymwegen with the Dutch. France had made substantial territorial gains, and, if Holland was not beaten, there was no telling when Louis might decide to march again. It was at this point that Titus Oates arrived on the scene, claiming that he had evidence of a Catholic conspiracy to murder the King and supplant him with the Duke of York. The horrors of the Popish Plot were about to begin.

I

The Plot first hatcht at Rom:
by the Pope and Cardinalls
&c.

II

S.ʳ E.B. Godfree takeing D.
Oates his depositions.

V

D.ʳ Oates receiues letters from
ÿ Fathers to carry beyond Sea.

VI

Coleman drawn to his
execution.

IX

The Seizing severall
Conspirators.

X

M.ʳ Langhorn deliuering out
Comissions for severall Offic.ˢ

Dr Oates discovereth Gauan in the Lobby.

Coleman giveth a Guiny to Incourage ye 4 Ruffians.

7 Damnable Plots 1678-85

Coleman examin'd in New: gate by severall Lords

Coleman writing a declaration and letter to la Chess.

The Irish Ruffians going for Windsor.

Mr Everard imprison'd in the Tower.

Dr Oates discovereth ye Plot to ye King and Councell.

THE HOT SUMMER OF 1678 strained the nerves of the highest and lowest in the land. Tension ran high, and in a super-stitious age the portents did not help. Three eclipses of the sun and two of the moon occurring in that single year were viewed apprehensively as signs of heavenly displeasure, while warnings from the astrologers and soothsayers appeared in unusually large numbers. 'Frenzies, inflamations and new infirmities proceeding from choleric humours', and 'troubles from great men and nobles' were themes of their disturbing predictions. It was a climate in which unease could all too naturally degenerate into madness.

On 13 August the King was taking his usual walk in St James's Park when Christopher Kirkby, who held a minor appointment in his laboratory, approached him in a state of agitation. 'Sire, your enemies have a design against your life. Keep within the company, for I know not but you may be in danger in this very walk', he said. 'How may that be?' asked Charles. 'By being shot at', answered Kirkby. Charles was unperturbed, sent Kirkby on his way and finished his walk in peace. He was quite used to such rumours, for wild talk of plots and conspiracies were commonplace enough in those anxious times. Besides, he was off to Windsor the following day and in no mood to be distracted by alarmist nonsense.

But while Charles was at Windsor the matter was not allowed to rest. Kirkby had acted as a go-between, and now the real authors of the plot – for it was indeed a work of fiction – came forward to claim the limelight. They were a strange pair: Israel Tonge, frail in figure, studious in aspect, biologist and cleric, whose chief occupation was the discovery of Jesuit conspiracies; and Titus Oates, squat, bull-necked, bow-legged, and with a jaw so enormous that his mouth appeared to be, hideously, in the middle of his face. Oates was a perjurer by profession, distinguished only by the scale of his activities from the host of rogues and adventurers who made their profit out of a society which knew no police force, no sophisticated methods of detection, and which depended on the sworn testimony of witnesses to bring culprits to justice. He had enjoyed a varied career: at one time as an Anglican clergyman, and at another a Jesuit; and by the time of the plot he was a good Anglican again, burning with zeal to denounce his former co-religionists. He

170

171

had tried hard to discover a real Jesuit plot, but having failed he suggested to Tonge that they should invent one and manufacture the evidence necessary to support it. Now they brought it to the attention of Danby, who showed every sign of concern at their claim to have discovered a conspiracy to dispose of the King in favour of the Duke of York. Possibly Danby thought there might have been some truth in what they said, or possibly he thought that the investigation might serve to improve his own highly insecure standing with Parliament. Whatever the reason, he became the plot's first distinguished patron. Twice he lay in wait at Windsor for the assassins who, Tonge assured him, were on their way. Extraordinarily enough some accident prevented their arrival on both occasions and Danby was left with nothing more tangible than the glib words of his informants.

Nevertheless the minister brought the affair before the Privy Council, and it was at a Council meeting that Charles first heard the full details of the alleged conspiracy after his return to the capital. Oates and Tonge were examined at a meeting which began on Saturday, 28 September, and lasted all the following day. Charles was present on the Sunday, and listened with astonishment as the marvellous tale was unfolded. The Pope was in the plot, as were the King of France, the General of the Jesuits, and the Archbishop of Dublin. In England five Catholic peers – Arundel, Powis, Petre, Stafford and Bellassis – were named as leaders, while at a given signal thousands of Catholic fanatics would rise to murder the honest Protestant citizens of London and the capital would be burned to the ground by an army of incendiaries. As to the assassination of the King, nothing was left to chance. He was to be waylaid by Irish ruffians; stabbed by Jesuits; shot with silver bullets in St James's Park; and poisoned by the Queen's physician.

Charles's reaction was, understandably, one of disbelief. He could not keep a straight face when told the bed-ridden Bellassis was to be the commander-in-chief of the Papist army. He put a few pertinent questions to Oates, proving to his own satisfaction that the whole story was pure fabrication, and promptly left for the cleaner air of Newmarket.

Yet in the King's absence the plot thrived, aided by two strokes of fortune. The first was the discovery of a bulky correspondence in which Edward Coleman, secretary to the

Duchess of York and a former secretary to the Duke, had engaged with a variety of prominent Catholics abroad, including two confessors of the French King. The letters made exciting reading. They were written in cypher, with code-names, such as the East India Company for Parliament, abounding – the very stuff of secrets and plots. Moreover they were certainly treasonable, looking forward to the growing influence of the Duke of York and the Catholics, to the elimination of Parliament, and to a supply of foreign money to make this possible. One of them, to Albani, the Papal Nuncio in Brussels, read:

> If the Duke can show to the King the true cause of all these misfortunes and persuade him to change the method of their trade, which he may easily do with the help of money, he will without difficulty drive away the Parliament and the Protestants who have ruined all their affairs for so great a time, and settle in their employments the Catholics, who understand perfectly well the nature of this sort of trade.

Such a correspondence was dangerous folly, and, though it was scarcely evidence of the elaborate plot worked out by Oates, it was enough to convince most people that something very sinister was afoot. Coleman was interrogated at length and urged to save his life by denouncing his fellow-conspirators. His pitiful cry that enough was known to condemn him but he did not know enough to be saved, proved to be no more than the truth. Coleman's guilt was assumed, and with it the reality of the plot. Everyone wondered when the Catholics would make their move, and little more was needed to engender wholesale panic.

That was forthcoming with the second of the unforeseen developments – the death of the London magistrate to whom Oates and his confederate had sworn their testimony. The fate of Sir Edmund Berry Godfrey remains one of history's great unsolved mysteries. On 12 October he disappeared from his home: five days later his body was found on Primrose Hill, the face badly bruised, swellings on the neck and a sword thrust right through the body. There was evidence that the sword had been inserted after death and there was some talk of suicide by hanging. But the overwhelming majority assumed the obvious: Godfrey had been murdered by Papists, and Tonge helped to

BABEL and BETHEL: or, The POPE in his Colou[r]

WITH

The Church of *ENGLAND's* Supplication to his Majefty, our gracious Soveraign, the true Defender of the F[aith]

To protect her from all the Machinations of *Rome*, and its bloody Emiffaries.

Rome's Scarlet whore doth here in Tryumph Ride,
And Spurns off Soveraign Crowns in Height of Pride
Poor Chriftians and brave Citties too fhee Burns
And Stabbs and Poifons daily ferve her Turns.

Behold our Church (like Efther here doth tend)
Her Supplication to the Faiths Defender
In vain Rome Plotts, whilft Charles ye Scepter Sway
May Sled and Gibbet end all Traitors Dayes.

An anti-Catholic broad-sheet, showing the Pope as Babel and Charles as Bethel, appealing to the King to support the English Church and stamp out Catholicism.
In the background, to the left, the horrors of Catholicism are shown.

confirm the obvious by turning the letters of the magistrate's name into 'Dy'd by Rome's reveng'd fury'. Almost overnight the capital was reduced to a state of hysteria. Houses were barricaded against the imminent Catholic rising; fine ladies like the Countess of Shaftesbury carried pistols in broad daylight for protection; Catholic houses were ransacked for secret caches of weapons; Popish books and relics were ferreted out and publicly burned; priests were hunted down; innocent suspects dragged off to prison. One man wrote that if anything Catholic appeared, even a dog or a cat, it would have been cut to pieces in a moment, while a commercially-minded cutler manufactured a special 'Godfrey' dagger with the words 'remember the murder of Edmund Berry Godfrey' engraved on one side, 'remember religion' on the other. Three thousand were sold in one day, to be carried by day, slept with by night to defend their owners against Godfrey's fate. Through London

174

the mobs marched, and the streets echoed with their shouts of 'No Popery!' From their headquarters at the King's Head tavern, Shaftesbury and the other members of the Green Ribbon Club urged on the good work, making the most of their unprecedented opportunity to attack the Duke of York, the friendship with France and the Popish policies of the King.

Charles was sickened by it all. On his return from Newmarket he examined Oates again more closely, tripping him up on several points of detail. But nothing could shake the public's faith in the man now elevated to the status of national saviour. Oates was installed in guarded apartments in Whitehall and given a State pension; his lightest word was now treated as the voice of revelation; his accusing finger enough to send innocent men and women to Newgate. Not surprisingly, others joined in the rich pickings to be earned for informing against Catholic conspirators. William Bedloe, perjurer and thief, was among them. He denounced a Catholic silversmith called Miles Prance who was unlucky enough to be overheard saying that Jesuits were honest men. Bedloe accused him of Godfrey's murder, and the poor man could prove no alibi. Thrown into Newgate, heavily manacled, execution awaiting him, near-demented with fear, Prance saved himself by admitting his guilt and implicating three other innocent men, Green, Berry and Hill. His state of mind may be judged by the fact that at various times he recanted his confession, before Charles in person, recanted his recantation, reaffirmed his original recantation and finally swore to the whole truth of his first confession. But his evidence was enough to condemn Green, Berry and Hill. Afterwards people marvelled to recall that in former times Primrose Hill had been known, of all things, as Greenberry Hill.

Such was the atmosphere of unreason and suspicion in which Parliament reassembled in the late autumn. Naturally the plot dominated everything. Charles refused to discuss it, 'lest I may seem to say too much or too little', but told the members that he would 'leave the matter to the law', thereby washing his hands of the fate of his Catholic subjects. He thus remained a passive spectator while Parliament deprived all Catholic peers, save only the Duke of York, from their places in the Upper House and busied itself with such resolutions as 'there hath been, and still is, a damnable and hellish plot for the assassinating and murdering of the King, and for subverting and rooting out and destroying the Protestant religion'.

The nation-wide agitation against Catholics affected the court deeply. James was restless and unhappy, and even Charles lost something of that easy-going affability which, even in his darkest moments, he had always managed to retain. Men noticed that he was irritable, given to sudden tempers and that sometimes his face would lose all colour in his rage. When, late in November, Oates had the temerity to accuse the Queen herself of being a party to the plot, even he was terrified into silence by the look which came into the King's face. In this crisis King and Queen were drawn closer together than they had ever been, and Catherine felt deeply her gratitude to the man who stood between her and her enemies.

> There is nothing [she wrote to her brother] that concerns me more than to tell you how completely the King releases me from all trouble . . . by the care which he takes to defend my innocence and truth. Every day he shows more clearly his purpose and good-will towards me, and thus baffles the hate of my enemies . . . I cannot cease telling you what I owe to his benevolence, of which each day he gives better proofs, either from generosity or from compassion, for the little happiness in which he sees I live.

From defending his Queen, Charles turned to the problem of saving his chief minister. Louis had never forgiven Danby for his part in the marriage between William and Mary and the Anglo-Dutch rapprochement. Now, in December, this enmity was dramatically translated into a *coup* against the minister. Ralph Montagu, England's former ambassador to Paris, was one of the Danby's most unrelenting opponents. He had recently been dismissed from his post and from the Privy Council, and was ready to take his revenge. Through the agency of Paul Barillon, the French ambassador in London, he suggested that he should reveal the correspondence relating to the last French subsidy, which, he was certain, would lead to Danby's immediate impeachment. As a reward for this service Louis was to pay him a pension. Charles and Danby were well aware of the danger, and on 19 December an extraordinary meeting of the Council took the decision to surround Montagu's house with King's men, and to confiscate his papers. But they were too late. Montagu had hidden the incriminating

176

documents with a friend, and announced to a shocked House of Commons: 'I believe that the seizing of my cabinet and papers was to get into their hands some letters of great consequence, that I have to produce, of the designs of a great Minister of State. That I have to produce.' The effect was electrifying. The House clamoured for the papers, and the cabinet, where the letters of great consequence were concealed, was brought in. It was locked, and a locksmith was sent for to break it open. Then Montagu took out his papers and handed them to the Speaker, who received the correspondence amid mounting excitement. Poor Danby had tried to protect himself. At the bottom of the draft of each letter were the words 'I approve of this letter, Charles R'. But his enemies were in no mood to listen to the niceties of his argument that he was carrying out lawful instructions. The letters were read out by the Speaker to a shocked House of Commons, and impeachment proceedings were begun. Early in the New Year Charles took the decision he had avoided for so long, and dissolved his Parliament. For the first time in eighteen years, writs were issued for new elections, and the well-organised Country Party set out to ensure by persuasion, bribery and intimidation that when the new Parliament met it would be dominated by their supporters.

'Let the blood lie on those that condemn them . . .'

The elections were fought amid the fury of the plot. Already it had claimed its first victims. Coleman was tried and executed in December. In February Green, Berry and Hill went to their deaths. The five Catholic peers accused by Oates were in the Tower. All over the country, the witch-hunt continued; suspects filled the prisons, among them a Mr Pepys, 'an elderly gentleman who had known softness and the pleasures of life', vulnerable because of his long career at the Admiralty under the Duke of York; it was said that thirty thousand Catholics fled from London alone to escape the persecution. The best that Charles could do was to exempt from the rigours of the law the Penderells, Father Huddlestone and the other Catholics who had saved his life. Otherwise he could do nothing. 'Let the blood lie on those that condemn them', said Charles, 'for God knows I sign with tears in my eyes.'

But Charles at least attempted to cool the political temperature. He urged his brother to abandon, or at least pretend to abandon, his faith. When James refused – after first consulting

ABOVE Sir Christopher Wren,
when he was President of the
Royal Society between 1680
and 1682. Painting by
J. B. Klosterman.

RIGHT St Paul's Cathedral,
perhaps Wren's greatest
architectural achievement,
although it was still incomplete
at his death in 1723.

178

his priests – he was sent, sullen and protesting, to Brussels. The King even brought his leading enemies into the Council, including such outspoken critics as Halifax and the Earl of Essex, while Shaftesbury himself was made Lord President. In London bonfires blazed as the citizens celebrated the apparent victory of the Country Party. But here they were deceived. Charles had no intention of allowing his opponents influence in the Council, and sought only to involve them in responsibility for his policies. 'Odd's fish', he remarked to an attendant, 'they have put a set of men about me, but they shall know nothing'.

In Parliament Shaftesbury and his colleagues continued their agitation. The elections had destroyed the formidable body of support for the court which Danby had so industriously built. Danby himself was sent to the Tower where he spent the next five years – at least in safety – periodically to be consulted by the King on affairs of State. Meanwhile the talk was all of exclusion. In April the Commons debated that: 'The Duke of York being a Papist and the hopes of his coming soon to the Crown have given the greatest countenance and encouragement to the present conspiracies and designs of Papists against the King and the Protestant religion'. Charles made it clear that he was willing to accept restrictions on a Catholic successor – to guarantee, in effect, a Protestant rule during a Catholic reign – but on the question of the succession itself he was quite adamant; James would not be excluded. Yet Parliament was not to be deterred. In May a resolution was carried 'that a bill be brought to disable the Duke of York to inherit the Imperial Crown of this realm' and when the Commons proceeded to debate the Exclusion Bill which followed, Charles prorogued and then dissolved his short-lived Parliament, saying: 'I will submit to anything rather than endure the gentlemen of the Commons any longer.' It had been a barren session. Only one Act had found its way onto the Statute Books, that of Habeas Corpus, traditionally regarded as the bulwark of English liberties. And even this only suceeded, it was said, because the members of the Upper House amused themselves by counting one very fat member as ten.

Charles now found himself deserted by almost all those who had been closest to him. Louise became alarmed at her increasing unpopularity and by Shaftesbury's threat to proceed against her as a 'common whore'. In self-defence she aligned herself with the all-powerful Earl, promising to use her influence with the King in favour of Exclusion. Even Nelly, celebrated by Londoners as 'the Protestant whore', supped with the King's enemies. But the crowning defection was that of Charles's eldest son, Monmouth, dazzled by the hopes of legitimacy and king-ship which Shaftesbury held before him. Monmouth had always been the King's favourite. He had been welcomed at court, showered with titles and commands. He was handsome, popular and capable. But, even for a son he adored, Charles would not set aside the rightful claims of a brother he despised. As Monmouth became the darling of the mobs, rejoicing in his role as the champion of the Protestants, and was seen to be omitting the bar sinister from his coat-of-arms, so he isolated himself increasingly from his saddened but still-loving father. In June 'the Protestant Duke', as he was acclaimed, achieved spectacular success in crushing a revolt of Scottish Covenanters at Bothwell Brig; a great military reputation was added to his laurels, and he was emerging daily as a growing threat to Charles's policies.

The plot was still raging in August when Charles suddenly fell ill. He had caught a chill taking a walk by the river after a hard game of tennis, and for a time his death seemed certain. His ministers were thrown into a panic, a measure of how close the country was to civil war. One thought that if the King died it would be 'the end of the world'. Henry Savile wrote to his brother Halifax 'the very thought of it frights me out of my wits'. James was hurriedly summoned from Brussels; but by the time he arrived, Charles had recovered, and was soon sitting up in bed, eating mutton and partridges and discussing his forthcoming visit to Newmarket.

But the ministers had had a shock. Some of them, like Halifax, began to reconsider their position, and slowly a body of support for the King's essentially reasonable stand began to develop among moderate men. Yet for the moment the restoration of sanity seemed as distant a prospect as ever. The extremists among the Exclusionists were pursuing a desperate course, past hope of compromise, in which their only alterna-tives were total victory or utter defeat. James was once more despatched to Brussels, though he was soon allowed to return

182

to Scotland where he found an outlet for his frustrations by tyrannising over the luckless Presbyterians. Monmouth, too dangerous to leave at large, was deprived of his commands and sent packing to Holland. On 17 November, the anniversary of Queen Elizabeth's accession, the Green Ribbon Club organised a massive demonstration of its strength. A long procession passed through the City, bearing effigies of the Pope, Godfrey and Jesuits with knives at the ready, accompanied by thousands of yelling 'brisk boys' whom Shaftesbury, now dismissed from the Council, regarded as his private army. Before the end of the month Monmouth was back in England to the rage of his father and the delight of the City who fêted him with an ostentation fitting for an heir to the throne. Rumours were circulated about a mysterious black box, said to contain papers proving that Charles had married Monmouth's mother. The King felt compelled to announce to a special meeting of the Council that he had never married anyone except his Queen, and the statement was duly published in the *Gazette*. Monmouth felt the humiliation bitterly, but did not abandon his hopes. And when, in October, Charles met his new Parliament, Shaftesbury, Monmouth and the Exclusionists prepared for a showdown. This time the Exclusion Bill passed the Commons and was sent up to the Lords where a fierce and prolonged debate took place. Shaftesbury led the attack for the Country Party. Opposing him was the reasoned eloquence of Halifax. Charles came down to the House, listening but never intervening as peer after peer rose to say his piece. Just once, when Monmouth spoke in favour, he was heard to murmur 'the kiss of Judas'. Halifax spoke sixteen times, and when the vote was taken, his persuasive arguments had won the day. The Bill was lost, and amid the storm of acrimony and abuse which followed, Charles quietly announced the close of the session. Moreover he felt strong enough to tell his Council that his next Parliament would meet in the traditional Royalist stronghold of Oxford.

For Charles the defeat of the Exclusion Bill was a considerable triumph and everywhere there were signs that at last opinion was turning in his favour. Juries were beginning to return acquittals for those accused even by Oates; Royalist pamphleteers were encouraged to answer the tirades of the Shaftesbury faction. At Oxford, Parliament would not be overawed by the

OPPOSITE James, Duke of Monmouth, the adored son of Charles II. As a Protestant, he plotted with Shaftesbury against the Catholic succession of his uncle James, Duke of York. He was extremely popular and quickly assumed the role of the champion of the Protestants.

On the anniversary of Elizabeth's accession, 17 November 1679, Shaftesbury organised a massive anti-Catholic procession to march through the City of London. The scene reconstructed the 'Popish Plot' with the Pope,

Jesuits with knives at the ready,
and other Catholic plotters
following the unfortunate Godfrey.

chanting of the London mobs outside their Houses. The plot had almost run its course; though not quite. There were still to be executions, including the aged and defenceless Stafford and the last of them, Archbishop Plunket of Armagh. But the waiting game Charles had played had been timed to perfection. His own personal popularity was undimmed – indeed it was one of the chief weapons exploited by the Exclusionists in their attacks on the Duke of York and those said to be plotting against the King. Now sentiments of loyalty to the King, the shame felt by many at their participation in recent events, and the natural waning of a movement too dependent on feverish anxiety to be sustained forever, had created an atmosphere more favourable than Charles had known for many years. It was noticed that he was unusually cheerful as he prepared to meet the final Parliament of his reign in March 1681.

Charles had good reason to be pleased. At last, after long negotiations, he had come to terms with Louis for a renewal of his subsidy. It was a return to the old policy, helped by the French King's realisation that exclusion might bring, not Monmouth, but his enemy William of Orange to the English throne. Charles was meeting a Parliament confident in the knowledge that he did not need it. For the Whigs, the Oxford Parliament was the last chance. They could not know what was in the King's mind and hoped that even now they might force through the Exclusion Bill and compel assent from their reluctant sovereign. Shaftesbury sought to make a show of force and the roads to Oxford were lined with his supporters flaunting their ribbons. Against them were drawn the lines of King's men. In Oxford, where the Commons met in Convocation House, the Lords in the Geometry School (now part of the Bodleian), the Country Party returned again to Exclusion. Shaftesbury demanded that Monmouth should be legitimised, and when Charles replied that to do this was against divine justice and the law of the land, the Earl told him that Parliament would attend to the alteration of the law. The King's reply was emphatic:

> My Lord [he said] let there be no self-delusion. I will never yield and will not let myself be intimidated. Men ordinarily become more timid as they grow old; as for me, I shall be, on the contrary, bolder and firmer and I will not stain my life and reputation in the

'*My Lord, let there be no self-delusion. I will never yield*'

186

little time that perhaps remains for me to live. I do not fear the dangers and calamities which people try to frighten me with. I have the law and reason on my side.

Then he turned to the assembled rows of Bishops, pointed, and declared: 'There is the Church, which will remain united with me.' There were no further attempts to reach a Parliamentary solution, and within a few days it was all over, the end accompanied by a little act of drama which Charles obviously enjoyed. On the night of Sunday, 27 March his coaches were discreetly sent out of Oxford to wait for him. On Monday morning he arrived at the Lords, apparently merely to listen, as was his custom, to their debate. But he was followed by a closed sedan chair in which were concealed his robes of State. Hurriedly he put them on, and summoned the Commons to attend. Wondering what was happening, but suspecting that the King was about to give way, the Commons filed in, their Exclusionist leaders swaggering in front. Charles made a brief, terse speech, and the astonished members were informed that they stood dissolved. The King was now in the best of moods. He placed his hand on the shoulder of an attendant, Thomas Bruce, and told him that he was better off with one King than five hundred. Then, after dining in the town, he drove hard for London.

Charles did not expect to have to meet Parliament again, and the Country Party, baffled at the moment of seeming success, wondered what the future now had in store for them. They did not have long to wait. Up and down the country a Royalist reaction gathered momentum. On 2 July Shaftesbury was taken from his bed for examination by the Council and despatched to the Tower. Though, to Charles's disappointment, he was acquitted by a London jury, the King was taking steps to ensure that such accidents would not recur. Boroughs were forced to surrender their charters, and Royalist mayors and sheriffs replaced their Whig predecessors. In the autumn Oates was removed from Whitehall and exchanged his luxurious quarters for a prison cell. The Crown's victory was complete. 'The Whigs come over to us daily', exulted one follower of the court. Shaftesbury tried desperately to rally his dwindling body of supporters. On Guy Fawkes Day he failed completely to rouse his once formidable 'brisk boys'; while on the anniversary

Broadsheet showing incidents from the Rye House Plot of 1683. The failure of this plot forced Monmouth to flee the country and enabled Charles to eliminate the leading Whigs who opposed him.

OT : Or, A Prospect of
Ends Miserable, Deaths Exemplary.

ısult, Hastens the Damnable Plot to be put in Execution.

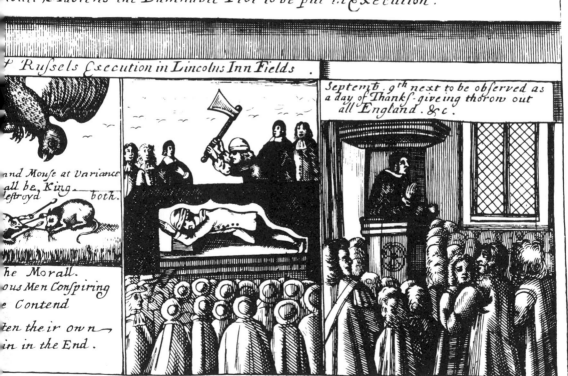

ꝑ Ruſsels Execution in Lincolns Inn Fields.

and Mouse at variance
all be, King
eſtroyd   both.

he Morall.
ous Men Conspiring
e Contend
ten their own
in in the End.

Septemb. 9ᵗʰ next to be obſerved as
a day of Thankſ-giveing thorow out
all England. &c.

of Elizabeth's accession, that greatest of Whig occasions, he attempted to mobilise his mob for the last time. Nothing happened. Tory sheriffs patrolled the empty London streets, ready for trouble if it came. Only at about three in the morning, in a back-yard near Bishopsgate, did they stumble on any sign of disturbance, 'a parcel of equivocal monsters, half-formed like the fable of the mud of the Nile: legs and arms scattered about, heads undressed and bodies beheaded'. Shaftesbury had no more to offer, and a few days later fled to Holland where he was shortly to die, broken in spirit and crippled with disease.

For the first time in a long while Charles had begun to enjoy life again. In the summer of 1682, he spent much of his time at sea, while he had discovered the pleasures of fishing which took up an increasing amount of his leisure. 'He will keep well if he can be kept from fishing when a dog would not be abroad', said one contemporary. In the autumn the King paid his usual visit to the races. He was ageing and no longer rode his own horses. But Sir John Reresby has left a delightful account of how Charles passed his time at Newmarket in his later years:

> The King was so much pleased with the country, and so great a lover of the diversions which that place did afford, that he let himself down from majesty to the very degree of a country gentleman. He mixed himself amongst the crowd, allowed every man to speak to him that pleased; went a-hawking in the mornings, to cock matches or foot races in the afternoons (if there were no horse-races), and to plays in the evenings acted by very ordinary Bartholomew Fair comedians.

In the spring of 1683 Charles was again at Newmarket, but on 22 March a fire destroyed many of the buildings including his own house. He therefore returned to London earlier than expected, and so avoided what might have been a tragic and peremptory ending to the reign. For the Exclusionists, though in eclipse, had not yet given up. Monmouth, together with such great Whig lords as Russell and Essex, and urged on by the dying Shaftesbury from exile, plotted treasonably against the Catholic succession. Meanwhile a small group of fanatics, led by an old Cromwellian soldier, was engaged in a more drastic conspiracy. Their plan centred on Rye House on the New-market road, from which they intended to ambush the royal party as it returned. Both Charles and his brother – now

PREVIOUS PAGES
The winter of 1683–4 was one of the coldest of the century, and the River Thames froze over. This painting by Abraham Hondius shows the Frost Fair created on the ice.

entrenched again among the leading Councillors – were to be assassinated and Monmouth proclaimed King. Foiled by the unexpected change in the King's movements, the conspiracy collapsed, and it was not long before some of the plotters sought to save themselves by turning informers. By the summer the whole story had been exposed; some of the plotters were executed, some fled into exile. More important, the Rye House conspiracy was used to eliminate many of the great Whig lords who, though followers of Monmouth, were not directly linked to the attempt on the King's life. In this way such prominent figures as Russell and Sidney were executed; and Essex committed suicide in his cell. Monmouth went into hiding, but, though a reward of £500 was offered for his capture, Charles did not try too hard to bring his son to justice.

The Rye House conspiracy was the last crisis of the reign, and with its passing the country settled into tranquillity. In August Charles went to Windsor, where 'it was all very quiet: a day's buck-hunting in the forest, a game of basset at the Queen's or crimp at the Duchess of Portsmouth's, or the wonders of the great water-engine Morland had built for the Castle, were the chief recreations the place afforded'. At the end of the month Charles moved his family to Winchester.

> Every day [wrote Sir Arthur Bryant] the King rode out at dawn on to the Downs to follow his hawks, cantering lazily with his red-coated falconers across the sea-like turf. Wren was building him a palace on the hill above the town: where the old castle had stood – a graceful, classical structure with a marble portico and colonnaded wings, and a cupola above, whence a King, who loved the Fleet of England, could see his men-of-war riding at Spithead. When it was finished, Charles told his guests, its tall windows would look down an avenue, two hundred feet wide, with noble houses on either side, and the long cathedral and the skyline of the Downs to close the vista. Here, in a capital worthy of his empire, he would spend his declining years, and future kings should call him blessed.

But there remained one wound: the breach with Monmouth. In great secrecy the King prepared the way for a reconciliation. Twice that autumn Monmouth visited his father at Whitehall and agreed to sign a document admitting his guilt; Charles agreed to pardon him. On 24 November the Duke surrendered himself, and the following day was received at court to the

Yacht race between the *Cleveland* and the *Henrietta* in about 1678. The *Cleveland* was Charles's own boat and the king did much to introduce yachting into England. Painting by Van de Velde.

King's undisguised delight. But his joy was not to last. Monmouth's friends persuaded him to reconsider, and under their
influence his resolution wavered. Then, quite suddenly, he
demanded back his confession. Charles was enraged and sent
an angry message telling him to 'go to hell': and soon his son
had fled the country into exile.

That winter was the coldest in living memory and Charles's
subjects amused themselves by building a town of tents on the
frozen Thames. With the coming of warmer weather the King
attended his last spring meeting at Newmarket, where he
walked in the mornings, watched races in the afternoons, went

196

Winchester Palace as it was envisaged by Sir Christopher Wren. After Charles's death the work ceased on what was to have been Charles's chief residence. The engraving is taken from Milner's *Survey of the Antiquities of Winchester*, published in 1816.

to plays in the evenings and supped with Louise. The Duchess of Portsmouth was now more than ever re-established as *maîtresse en titre*, and it was noticed how Charles's fondness for her 'increased very much, and broke out in very indecent instances'. The old acrimony amongst the mistresses had died away, and Louise, Nelly and Hortense all fitted easily into the quiet routine of the middle-aged King. There was little to disturb the calm of his days, except the occasional domestic anxiety, such as that which occurred when the Grand Prior of France had the temerity to start making love to Louise. Charles's jealous instincts, which he had rarely shown as a younger man, were immediately aroused; and his rival was ordered to leave the country.

Yet all through 1684 Charles's thoughts were increasingly about his son across the waters. Once again he sought a reconciliation, and messages passed between them. At the end of November 1684 the cloaked figure of the wayward Duke was glimpsed at Whitehall. What passed between him and his father is not known, but late the following month a letter reached him to say that he would be welcome to return the following February.

The year closed happily for Charles. His government was in the hands of such able servants as the 'Great Trimmer' Halifax. He was secure on his throne and in the harmony of his domestic circle. His subjects were prospering as never before from England's long peace while her European rivals were at war. All over the globe English seamen were building an Empire and capturing the trade routes. With an expanding trade came an expanding Crown revenue, and Charles was able to pay off some of his debts, even some of his father's. He had presentiments about the future, saying: 'I am weary of travelling and am resolved to go abroad no more. But when I am dead and gone I know not what my brother will do: I am much afraid that when he comes to wear the crown he will be obliged to travel again. And yet I will take care to leave my kingdoms to him in peace, wishing he may long keep them so. But this hath all of my fears, little of my hopes and less of my reason.'

Such fears seemed remote. Charles was not yet fifty-five, in good health and looking forward to the progress of his palace at Winchester and the approaching return of his son.

8
Death
and
Beyond
1685

ON SUNDAY, 1 FEBRUARY, Charles spent a relaxed and happy day. He was troubled by a sore foot, and was unable to take his customary morning walk; but he rode in his coach, dined well and paid a brief visit to Louise in the evening. It was the turn of his favourite gentleman-in-waiting, young Thomas Bruce, to lie with him in his Bedchamber; and it is to Bruce that we owe a meticulously detailed account of what followed.

As the King was escorted to his room the candle held for him went out, though there was not a breath of wind to account for it. Bruce thought it a bad omen, but Charles took no notice and chatted easily as he prepared for bed. 'As soon as he had put on his nightgown', wrote Bruce, 'he went to ease himself, and often more out of custom than necessity, by reason nobody would come in there but the gentleman and groom-in-waiting; and there he laughed and was most merry and diverting.' King and courtier talked of many things: Bruce seized the chance to ask for a place in the guards for one of his relatives, and was told that the colonel would surely grant the request; Charles discussed his palace at Winchester, saying: 'I shall be so happy this week to have my house covered with lead.' Then the two settled down for the night, Bruce to lie awake amid the many disturbances which everyone in his position was subjected to:

> Several circumstances made the lodging very uneasy – the great grate [being] filled with scotch coal that burnt all night, a dozen dogs [that] came to our bed, and several pendulums that struck at the half, quarter, and all not going alike it was a continual chiming. The King being constantly used to it, it was habitual.

But that night even Charles tossed restlessly in his bed, and in the morning he was clearly ill, his face drained of colour and his speech impaired. Nevertheless, the business of the day commenced normally, and the doors were opened to his barber and to Dr King who was attending his lame foot. The King settled himself in his usual chair and the barber began to fix the linen for his shave. Suddenly Charles slumped into Bruce's arms 'in a most violent fit of apoplexy'. Alarmed messengers rushed out to bring help, and Dr King, with great daring, drew sixteen ounces of blood, knowing well that he could have been hanged for doing so without orders from the Council. The Duke of York hurried in, wearing one shoe and one slipper, and Charles

A
TRUE RELATION
OF THE
Late Kings Death.

ON Monday, *being the* 2d. *of* February, *the* King *rose early,
saying, that he had not slept well the last Night: And about
seven of the Clock, coming from his private Devotions, out of his
Closet, fell down, (and scarce any sign of of Life remaining in him for
the space of four Houres) of a Fit of an Apoplexy, but with the loss
of sixteen Ounces of Blood, and other Aplications, came again to his
Sences, and great Hopes were of his Recovery, till* Thursday *one of
the* Clock*; so that at five, the Doctors being come before the* Council,
declared that the K--- *was in great Danger ; and on* Friday, *a quarter
before twelve, he departed this Life.* God have Mercy on his Soul.

P. M. A. C. F. came to the D. upon the Doctors telling him of the State of the K. and
tould him *that now was the time for him to take care of his Br. Soul,* and that it was his Duty to tell
him so : The D. with this Admonishment went to the K. and after some private Discourse,
the K. uttered these Expressions, *Oh B. how long have I wished—— but now help me* ; withal
declaring that he would have Mr. H. who had preserved him in the Tree, and now hoped
would preserve his Soul. Mr. *Hud.* was accordingly sent for, and desired to bring all Nes-
sisaries for a dying Man, but he not having the blessed Sacrament by him, went to one of
the Q. P. and telling him the Occasion, desired his Assistance to procure it, and to bring it to
the back Stairs. The K. having notice that Mr. H. waited at the Door, desired to be in
private, whereupon the Bps. and all the Nobles withdrew, the D. catching fast the Door,
the Lords P. B. and F. were going out also, but the D. told them that they might stay. The
K. seeing Mr. H. cryed out, *Almighty God, what good Planet governs me, that all my Life is
Wonders and Miracles ? When, O Lord, I consider my Infancy, my Exile, my Escape at* Worcester, *my Preservation in the Tree, with the Assistance of this good Father ; and now to have him again to preserve my
Soul : O Lord, my wonderful Restoration, my great Danger in the late Conspiracy ; and last of all, to
be raised from Death to Life, and to have my Soul preserved by the Assistance of this Father, whom I
see, O good Lord, that thou hast created for my Good.* The D. and Lords withdrew into the Clos-
set for the space of an houre and half, then entring again the Room, the F. asked the K.
whether he would be pleased to receive ; he answered, *If I were worthy of it* — Amen, Amen.
The F. remaining comforting and praying with him, he said, Father if I am worthy of it,
I pray let me have it ? The F. said it would be brought to him imediately, and asked his
Leave to proceed with extream Unction, the K. reply'd, with all my Heart, the D. and
Lords assisting at the time. Mr. H. was called to the Door, where he received the blessed
Sacrament, and desiring the K. to compose himself to receive, he would fain have arose
(but was perswaded to the contrary) saying, *Let me meet my heavenly Father in a better manner than lying on my back.* But being overruled, they continue in Prayer : Amongst others,
the Father repeats an Act of Contrition, desiring the K. to repeat it word by word after
him : Having made an end, the K. received with the greatest Expressions of Devotion
imaginable : This being ended, they go on with the Prayers *de Animæ* ; that being done,
the K. desired the Act of Contrition to be again repeated, saying, *O Lord, good God,
when my Lips fail, let my Heart speak these Words Eternally,* Amen. The Bishops and Lords
enter again the Room, and desire the K. to remember his last End, and to endeavour to
make a good End ; he said he had thought of it, and hoped he had made his Peace with
God ; they asked him whether he would receive, he said he would not ; so persisting in
Extolling the Q. and D. saying he was not sorry to leave the World, leaving so good a
Bro. her to Rule behind him.

F I N I S.

took Bruce's hand, murmuring 'I see you love me dying as well as living'. Charles was helped back to his bed, and soon more physicians were at his side. By now authority had been obtained, and they busily started further bleedings, and such other cures as were known to their primitive medical arts. All manner of potions were forced down the King's throat, and red–hot blistering agents applied to his head and body to keep him from losing consciousness. All that day, and all through Tuesday and Wednesday, the ministrations continued, though with diminishing hope that the patient would recover. Charles bore it all with astonishing humour, even attempting to joke with those keeping the vigil. 'I am sorry gentlemen, for being such an unconscionable time a–dying', he said.

On Thursday the King's condition worsened. Outside the palace ordinary men and women waited anxiously for news. In the churches, packed congregations continued to pray that even now his life might be spared. But Charles was close to death, and his churchmen were thinking of his immortal soul. They urged him to receive the last sacrament in the Anglican rite, but Charles waved them aside telling them there was time enough for that. Far away in her own apartments Louise knew better than the clerics what religious consolation her royal lover needed. It was not fitting for the mistresses to attend his bedside, but she sent word to James that his brother had secretly embraced their own, Catholic faith. Soon James was with the King whispering earnestly in his ear, offering to find him a priest and at last making him understand. 'For God's sake, brother, do, and please lose no time', whispered Charles. James immediately left the chamber, and to everyone's surprise the room was cleared save for two Protestant but completely trustworthy attendants. When James reappeared he was accompanied by the disguised figure of Father Huddlestone, now an old man, the priest who had assisted the King before in those far–off days of adventure and peril after Worcester. 'You that have saved my body, is now come to save my soul', said Charles. The King's peace with his new Church was quickly made. His confession was heard, and absolution given. Then Charles received the sacrament of extreme unction, and Father Huddlestone, rejoicing in his heart for the new convert, passed down the back stairs which had figured so prominently in happier times.

Now the throng outside were allowed back into the room, and last farewells were made. The grieving Queen was so overcome that she had to be assisted back to her room from where she sent word to her husband begging forgiveness for any wrongs she had done him. 'Alas, poor woman', was Charles's reply, 'she beg my pardon? I beg hers with all my heart: take back to her that answer.' The King's sons knelt before him for his blessing: Barbara's Southampton, Grafton and Northumberland: Nelly's St Albans and Louise's Richmond. The first and best loved of them all was not present.

In the early hours of Friday morning Charles took his leave of James, entreating him to look after Louise and his children. 'And let not poor Nelly starve', he added. By daybreak the King was scarcely conscious, and shortly afterwards lapsed into a coma, breathing noisily and with obvious difficulty. At about midday the breathing stopped, and James, the new sovereign of three kingdoms, bustled out to attend to his affairs. The room emptied, until at last only Bruce was left to watch that day and night over the corpse of his master.

'And let not poor Nelly starve'

With Charles died the age he had created. One by one those who had shared his peculiarly individual kingship departed from the scene. Barbara was already in France; Louise hastily followed, to live on for almost fifty years; Nelly survived her King for only two years; while the Queen returned to Portugal to find happiness as a wise and benevolent regent for two decades. Hortense alone stayed on in London, her salon the focus of scholars, wits and brilliant conversation as in times of old. Most of Charles's children spent their lives in quiet obscurity; except for Grafton, who died a hero's death in the storming of Cork in 1690, and Monmouth who went to the scaffold for his reckless attempt to seize by force the throne his father had denied him. James fulfilled his brother's prophecy and went into exile after a short and disastrous reign. He was succeeded by William of Orange and Mary, thus ensuring that England would, after all, have a Protestant monarchy.

Charles's death left a nation mourning for its loss, though the obsequies were brief and perfunctory. There was no lying in State, no elaborate funeral. Only a modest procession accompanied the coffin on its journey by night to Westminster

ABOVE A portrait of John
Milton (1608–74) painted
by W. Fairthorne. His
masterpiece, *Paradise Lost*,
was published in 1667.
RIGHT The frontispiece of
a later edition of
Paradise Lost.

Abbey. There the body was lowered into a tomb which, for two centuries, was not even distinguished by a name.

Yet Charles needed no monument to perpetuate his memory. Englishmen were soon looking back nostalgically to the 'Golden Days' which had passed with his death. As he had been the most popular of monarchs in his lifetime, so he lived on in the affections of generations who never knew him. For many years his Restoration was celebrated as Oak-apple Day in thanksgiving for his miraculous deliverance after Worcester. Inns up and down the country still carry his picture outside *The King's Head* or *The Black Boy*. It is not easy to account

BELOW The title page and frontispiece of John Bunyan's *Pilgrim's Progress*, first published in 1678. Like *Paradise Lost*, this masterpiece belonged in time, if not in spirit, to Charles's reign.

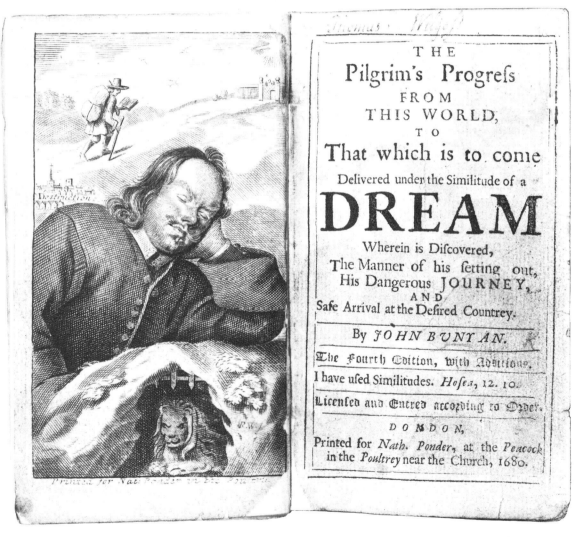

LEFT The easy-going
tolerance of the King and
his court gave fresh
impetus to poets and
dramatists such as John
Dryden (1631–1700).

for it all, except to say that he was above all the most human of kings. The Charles we remember best is the man among his jockeys at Newmarket; chatting with Nelly at the theatre; outpacing his breathless companions in the park; experimenting with his glasses and chemicals; fondling that breed of spaniel which still carries his name; and showing to the greatest and humblest of his subjects alike the same unfailing familiarity and courtesy.

Such intangibles count more for his popularity than the positive achievements of his reign, though these are remarkable enough. He inherited a monarchy weakened by civil war, restricted by legislation and overshadowed by his father's execution. He left it well-nigh absolute: unchallenged in government, supreme in law, and triumphantly solvent.

Charles was fortunate in being served by two men who founded the English school of portraiture – Sir Peter Lely (1618–80) and Sir Godfrey Kneller (1648–1723). Both were born in Germany, but lived and worked for most of their lives in England.
LEFT Sir Peter Lely who came to England in 1641 and was appointed State Painter and knighted by Charles.
RIGHT Sir Godfrey Kneller; he came to England in 1674 at the invitation of the Duke of Monmouth and was appointed Court Painter by Charles – a post which he held until his death.

S.ᴿ ISAAC NEWTON

Keeping the nation at peace while others were at war he enabled his subjects to lay the foundations of a prosperity which would, in the eighteenth and nineteenth centuries, make England a commercial, financial and industrial centre of the world.

Of the creative achievements of the reign there can be no doubt, though here the King's own responsibility is hard to define. Royal patronage was extended to Wren, Purcell, Lely and Dryden. Charles encouraged the spectacular development of the theatre, and many of the brilliant offerings of Restoration dramatists reflected the taste of the King and his court. But Charles not only encouraged those he admired: he refused to interfere with those whose ideas and inclinations were very different from his own. Such disapproving figures as Milton and John Bunyan were allowed to pursue their arts in peace, and *Paradise Lost* and *Pilgrim's Progress* belong in time, if not in spirit, to his reign. Tolerance is, indeed, the key to much of Charles's contribution to his age. It was not, of course, complete; but, holding few principles himself, Charles was, on the whole, not prepared to see other men's prejudices imposed on his dissenting subjects. Such an attitude stemmed naturally from the King's own curious and enquiring mind. The French traveller Sorbière noted how 'persons of quality' were applying themselves to 'chemistry, mechanism, mathematics or natural philosophy', and added, 'the King himself has been so far from being neglectful of these things, that he has attained to such knowledge as had made me astonished when I had audience with His Majesty'. The crowning glory of the new spirit was the Royal Society, whose activities went far beyond scientific research in the narrow sense. They included enquiries into trade, agriculture, shipbuilding, the weather, grammar, history, navigation; and even monsters and longevity. Among the members were many of the most illustrious figures of the age; Boyle, Hooke and Newton; Dryden, Wren and Locke; Buckingham, Evelyn and Pepys. The Society was both a centre for research and a forum for discussion, and though Charles did not always understand what its members were doing – he made fun of their attempts to weigh air, for example – he was an unfailing and enthusiastic supporter.

Of course there were less pleasant aspects to the reign. Evelyn summed up his own feelings of disillusionment:

OPPOSITE An engraving of Sir Isaac Newton, the greatest scientist of the age, by J. Honbraker from a painting by Sir Godfrey Kneller.

209

The Spirit of Enquiry

One of the most striking features of the years after 1660 was the widespread interest in and pursuit of scientific knowledge. With the active encouragement of the King, men such as Isaac Newton, Robert Boyle, Edmund Halley and Robert Hooke, discovered many of the principles which are fundamental to modern astronomy, chemistry, and physics. Centre of the ferment of activity was the Royal Society, founded in 1660, whose interests included enquiries into trade, agriculture, shipbuilding, meteorology, grammar, history and navigation.

BELOW Robert Boyle (1627–91), who conceived the principle of chemical elements and whose researches into the properties of air gave rise to 'Boyle's Law', one of the foundations of chemistry.

LEFT The Castlemaine
Globe from the Whipple
Science Museum in
Cambridge. This globe is
supposed to have been
used by Charles himself.

RIGHT An engraving by
I. Simon of the Greenwich
Observatory which was
founded by Charles. It is
from here that 'Greenwich
Mean Time' is calculated,
and from its meridian that
longitude is reckoned.

A painting by Thomas
Danckerts of Mr Rose,
the royal gardener,
presenting Charles with
the first pineapple
successfully raised in
England.

John Evelyn, whose diary covering the period 1640–1706 is an invaluable chronicle of contemporary events. Nevertheless he disapproved strongly of the tone of Charles's court.

God was incensed to make his reign very troublesome and unprosperous by wars, plagues, fires, loss of reputation by a universal neglect of the public for the love of a voluptuous and sensual life, which a vicious court had brought into credit. I think of it with sorrow and pity when I consider how good and debonair a nature that unhappy prince was: what opportunities he had to make himself the most renown'd King that ever swayed the British sceptre.

Evelyn was not alone. Disenchantment and a sense of lost op-

Samuel Pepys, one of the King's most able civil servants, whose diary from 1660 to 1669 provides much of the gossip and background which Evelyn ignored.

portunities is a theme which runs through many of the writings of those who greeted the Restoration with such hopes. At war Charles was inglorious, at peace often ignominious. During his reign standards of public life deteriorated with the example set by the King and court. Honesty, hard work and integrity were virtues which became increasingly rare. The moral standards of Charles and his courtiers were a source of scandal throughout the reign, and here the King never understood the gulf which separated his lax and self-indulgent court from the attitudes of

215

the broad mass of his subjects, and constantly underestimated their very genuine fears. To this extent he must take his share of the blame for a reaction which showed itself at its worst in the insanity of the Popish plot.

But when everything is said, Charles's achievement remains. Alone among the Stuarts he retained the common touch. Where men of high principle – his father, brother, and Oliver Cromwell among them – opened wounds, Charles, in his very personal way, was able to bide his time and wait. To a degree he succeeded where a greater or a lesser man would have failed. Perhaps it was as well that between the violence of civil war and the catastrophe of the reign of James II England had the prince described by Halifax, who 'might more properly be said to have gifts than virtues, as affability, easiness of living', and, most important of all, 'inclinations to give and to forgive'.

Select bibliography

Airy, Osmund, *Charles II* (1904)

Ashley, Maurice, *England in the Seventeenth Century 1603–1714* (1952)
  Charles II: The Man and the Statesman (1971)

Belloc, Hilaire, *The Last Rally: A Story of Charles II* (1940)

Bosher, R. S., *The Making of the Restoration Settlement* (1951)

Brett, A. C. A., *Charles II and His Court* (1910)

Browning, Andrew, *Thomas Osborne, Earl of Danby and Duke of Leeds 1632–1714* (1944–51)

Bryant, Arthur, *King Charles II* (rev. ed., 1955)
  Restoration England (rev. ed., 1960)
  The Letters, Speeches, and Declarations of King Charles II (1935)
  Samuel Pepys (3 vols, 1933–8)

Chapman, H. W., *The Tragedy of Charles II* (1964)

Cheruel, P. A. (ed.), *Mémoires de Mlle de Montpensier* (1858)

Clarendon, Earl of, *The History of the Rebellion and Civil Wars in England*, ed. W. D. Macray (1888)
  The Life of Edward, Earl of Clarendon (1827, among other editions)

Clark, G. N., *Science and Social Welfare in the Age of Newton* (1937)
  The Seventeenth Century (2nd ed., 1947)
  The Later Stuarts (2nd ed., 1956)
  The Wealth of England 1496–1760 (1946)

Coward, B., *The Stuart Age* (1980)

Davies, Godfrey, *The Restoration of Charles II 1658–1660* (1955)

Drinkwater, John, *Mr Charles, King of England* (1926)

Evelyn, John, *Diary*, ed. E. S. de Beer (6 vols, 1955)

Feiling, Keith, *British Foreign Policy 1660–1672* (1930)

Foxcroft, H. C., *A Character of the Trimmer* (1946)

Antonia Fraser, *King Charles II* (1979)

Haley, K. D. H., *The First Earl of Shaftesbury* (1968)

Hardacre, Paul H., *The Royalists during the Puritan Revolution* (1956)

Hartmann, C. H., *Clifford of the Cabal* (1937)

Hill, Christopher, *The Century of Revolution 1603–1714* (1961)

Hutton, Ronald, *Charles II: King of England, Scotland, and Ireland* (1989)
  The Restoration: A Political and Religious History of England and Wales 1658–1667 (1985)

Jones, J. R., *Charles II: Royal Politicians* (1987)

Jordan, W. K., *The Development of Religious Toleration in England* (1932–40)

Kenyon, J. P., *Robert Spencer, Earl of Sunderland* (1958)
  The Stuarts (1958)
  The Stuart Constitution (2nd ed., 1986)

Lee, Maurice, *The Cabal* (1965)

Loth, David G., *Royal Charles* (1931)

Matthews, William, *Charles II's Escape from Worcester* (1967)

Miller, John, *Charles II* (1991)

Ogg, David, *England in the Reign of Charles II* (1934)

Ollard, Richard, *The Escape of Charles II* (1966)

    The Image of the King: Charles I and Charles II (1979)

Pearson, Hesketh, *Charles II: His Life and Likeness* (1960)

Pepys, Samuel, *Diary*, ed. R. C. Latham and W. Matthews (11 vols, 1970–83

    The Illustrated Pepys, ed. R. C. Latham (1978)

Petrie, Charles, *The Stuarts* (1937)

Pollock, John, *The Popish Plot* (1903)

Rogers, P. G., *The Dutch in the Medway* (1970)

Scott, Lord George, *Lucy Walter: Wife or Mistress?* (1947)

Trevelyan, G. M., *England under the Stuarts* (21st ed., 1949)

Underdown, David, *Royalist Conspiracy in England 1649–1660* (1960)

Westfall, R. S., *Science and Religion in Seventeenth-Century England* (1958)

Willey, B., *The Seventeenth-Century Background* (1934)

Wilson, Charles, *Profit and Power: A Study of England in the Dutch Wars* (1957)

Witcombe, D. T., *Charles II and the Cavalier House of Commons 1663–1674* (1966)

Acknowledgments

Photographs and illustrations were supplied or are reproduced by kind permission of the following. The pictures on pages 10–11, 12, *14–15*, 32, 35, 46–7, *50–1*, 57/1, 68, 81, 88, 93, 100, 145, 156, 157 are reproduced by gracious permission of H.M. the Queen; on page 132 by kind permission of the Earl of Bradford; on pages 212–3 by kind permission of the Marchioness of Cholmondeley; on pages *62–3* by courtesy of His Grace the Duke of Roxburgh; on pages 66–7 by courtesy of the Duke of St Albans; on page *128/1* by kind permission of the Earl Spencer; on page 128/2 by kind permission of Lord Talbot de Malahide. Agnews: 212–3; Ashmolean Museum, Oxford: 19/2; D.E. Bower Collection, Chiddingstone, Kent: 78, 79, *128/3*; The Bowes Museum: 55, British Museum: 16–17; 33/1; 43/1, 43/2, 49, 60–1, 76–7, 85, 91, 101, 110–1, 134–5, 146–7, 162, 163, 168–9, 171 174; BPC: *3*, 60–1, 85, *113/1, 113/2*, 126–7, *128/1*, 214; Christchurch, Oxford: 214; Cromwell Museum: 58; Courtauld Institute of Art: 118/1, 123, 135, 138/1; Mary Evans: 19/1, 42; Trustees of the Will of the late J.M.C. Evelyn: 214; Werner Forman: *179*; John Freeman: 16–17, 33/2, 43/1, 43/2, 73, 76–7, 91, 110–11, 118/2, 134–5, 147, 168–9, 171, 174, 188–9, 204/2, 205, 211/3; Giraudon: 150–1; Guildhall Art Gallery: *113/2*, 115, 118/2; Miss Jennifer Horle: 126–7; Keystone: 72; London Museum: 23, 27, *190–1*; Longman Group Ltd.: *62–3*, 163, *190–1*; Mansell Collection: 70–1, 83, 86–7, 96–7, 111, 114, 120–1, 184–5, 201; Middle Temple: 123; Johan Maurits van Nassau Collection: 80; National Galleries of Scotland: 18; National Maritime Museum: 104, 106–7, 108; National Monuments Record (Crown Copyright): 119, 136; National Portrait Gallery: 26, 38, 57/2, *116*, *125*, 138/2, 138–9, 139/1, 139/2, 159, 204/1, 206/2, 207, 210/1, 215; Pepys Library, Magdalene College, Cambridge: 103; Radio Times Hulton Picture Library: 34, 36–7, 82, 182, 206/1; Rijksmuseum: 98; Royal Academy of Arts: 131, 132, 194–5; Royal Hospital, Greenwich: 164–5; Royal Society: *178*; Science Museum: 75, 208; Victoria and Albert Museum: *3*, 64, 140–1, 198; Walker Art Gallery, Liverpool: *2*; Warwick Castle Resettlement: 131; Whipple Science Museum, Cambridge: 210/2.

Picture research by Jane Dorner.

Index

Crofts, Lord, 54
Crofts, James, *see* James, Duke of Monmouth
Cromwell, Oliver, 25, 31, 40, 42, 44, 45, 53, 54, 56, 57, 59, 84
Cromwell, Richard, 59
Culpepper, Sir John, 27

Danby, Earl of, 155, 158, 160, 166, 167, 172, 176, 177, 180
Davies, Moll, 133
Dover, secret treaty of, 142, 144, 148, 155
Dryden, John, 109, 133, 160, 209
Dunbar, Battle of, 42, 44, 45

Edgehill, Battle of, 25
Elizabeth, Princess (sister of Charles II), 13
Etheredge, Sir George, 160
Essex, Earl of, 180, 192, 193
Evelyn, John, 22, 31, 69, 84–5, 112, 115, 143, 209, 214
Exclusion crisis, 166, 180, 181, 186, 187, 192

Fitzcharles, Charles, 56
Fitzroy, Charlotte, 56

Godfrey, Sir Edmund Berry, 173, 174, 175
Grafton, Duke of, 203
Graham, James, *see* Montrose, Marquis of
Grammont, Comte de, 149
Grandison, Lord, 65
Great Fire of London, 109–10, 115
Green, 175, 177
Green Ribbon Club, 158, 175, 183
Grenville, Sir John, 59
Gwynne, Nell, 129, 133, 136, 144, 161, 181, 197, 203, 207

Habeas Corpus, 180
Halifax, Marquis of, 160, 180, 181, 183, 197, 216

Hampden, John, 21
Hampton Court, 83, 90, 105
Harrison, Major-General, 84
Harvey, William, 25
Henrietta Maria, Queen of England, 13, 20, 25, 29, 39, 79, 80
Henrietta, Princess, *see* Minette
Henry, Duke of Gloucester, 13, 82
Hertford, Marquis of, 19
Hill, 175, 177
Hobbes, Thomas, 30
Hooke, Robert, 209
Hopton, Ralph, Lord, 27
Huddlestone, Father John, 48, 52, 177, 202
Hyde, Anne, 79, 80, 82
Hyde, Edward, *see* Clarendon, Earl of

Indulgence, Declaration of (1672), 145, 152, 153
Ireland, 39, 40, 41, 56
Ireton, Henry, 84

Jaffray, Alexander, 41
James, Duke of Monmouth, 31, 35, 40, 54, 105, 130, 181, 183, 186, 192, 193, 196, 197, 203
James, Duke of York, 13, 56, 65, 94, 101, 109, 122, 133, 148, 152, 158, 159, 166, 167, 181, 183, 186, 200, 202, 203; and the Civil War, 25, 31; and Anne Hyde, 79, 80, 82; and Mary of Modena, 154; and the Rye House Plot, 192–3
Jermyn, Henry, 1st Earl of St Albans, 30
Jersey, 28, 29, 40, 41

Kéroualle, Louise de, Duchess of Portsmouth, 142–3, 144, 154, 161, 166, 180–1, 197, 200, 202, 203
Killigrew, Betty, 56
King, Dr, 200
Kirkby, Christopher, 170

'La Belle Stewart', *see* Stewart, Frances
'La Grande Mademoiselle', *see* Orléans, Anne-Marie-Louise d'
Lane, Colonel, 52
Lane, Jane, 52, 53, 68
Laud, William, Archbishop of Canterbury, 13, 21, 24
Lauderdale, Duke of, 137, 142, 145, 154
Lely, Sir Peter, 209
Leslie, David, 42, 45
Locke, John, 209
London, 20, 25, 63, 101, 102, 104, 105, 109–10, 112, 115, 117, 154, 172, 174–5, 180, 187, 192
Lorraine, Chevalier de, 143
Louis XIV, King of France, 29, 77, 105, 137, 142, 143, 148, 149, 153, 158, 161, 163, 166, 167, 176, 186

Mancini, Hortense de, 161, 197, 203
Marston Moor, Battle of, 25
Marvell, Andrew, 74
Mary of Modena, 154, 173
Mary, Princess of Orange (sister of Charles II), 13, 65, 79, 82
Mary, Princess (daughter of James, Duke of York), 65, 166, 176, 203
May, Bab, 122
Mazarin, Cardinal de, 29, 54, 161
Milton, John, 209
Minette, 79, 99, 101, 117, 137, 142, 143, 149
Monck, George, *see* Albemarle, Duke of
Monmouth, Duke of, *see* James, Duke of Monmouth
Montagu, Ralph, 176–7
Montrose, Marquis of, 30–1, 39, 40, 41
Morland, Sir Samuel, 193

223

13.